Design For Embroidery:
A Fine Art Approach

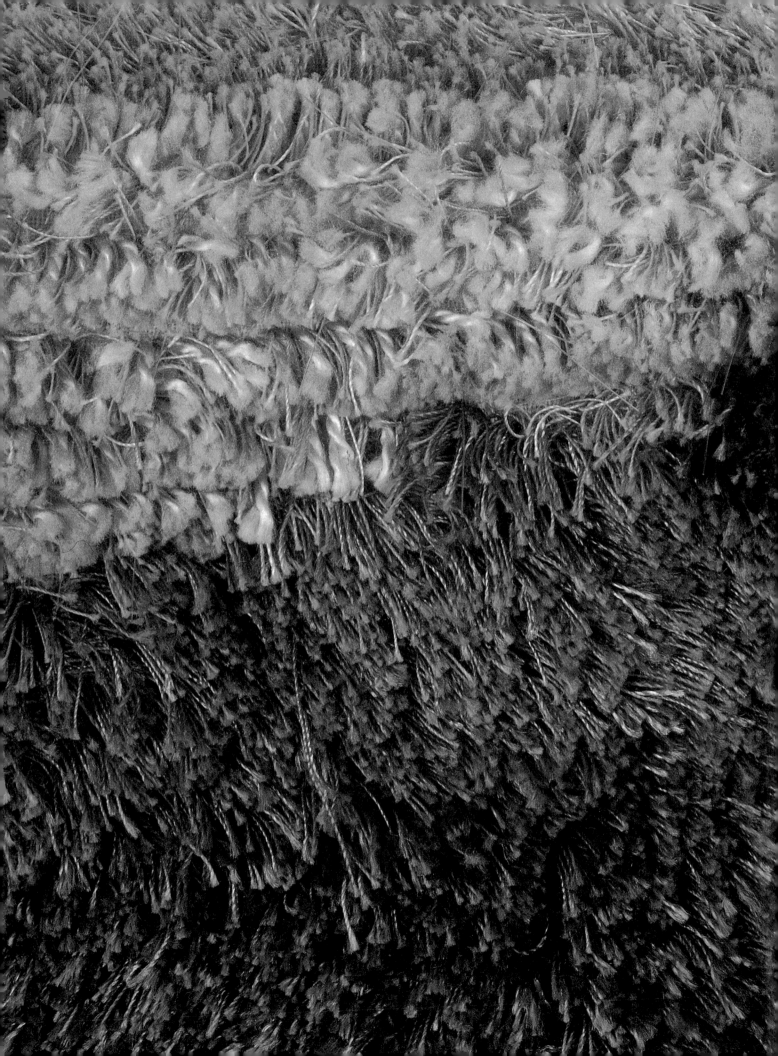

DESIGN FOR EMBROIDERY:

A FINE ART APPROACH

DIANA SPRINGALL

PELHAM BOOKS

PELHAM BOOKS
Published by the Penguin Group
27 Wrights Lane, London W8 5TZ, England
Viking Penguin Inc., 40 West 23rd Street, New York, New York 10010, USA
Penguin Books Australia Ltd, Ringwood, Victoria, Australia
Penguin Books Canada Ltd, 2801 John Street, Markham, Ontario, Canada L3R 1B4
Penguin Books (NZ) Ltd, 182–190 Wairau Road, Auckland 10, New Zealand

Penguin Books Ltd, Registered Offices: Harmondsworth, Middlesex, England

First published 1988

Copyright © 1988 Diana Springall

All rights reserved. Without limiting the rights under copyright reserved
above, no part of this publication may be reproduced, stored
in or introduced into a retrieval system, or transmitted, in any form
or by any means (electronic, mechanical, photocopying,
recording or otherwise), without the prior written permission of both
the copyright owner and the above publisher of this book.

Made and printed in Italy by Olivotto

Typeset by Cambridge Photosetting Services

British Library Cataloguing in Publication Data
Springall, Diana
  Design for embroidery.
  I. Embroidery
  I. Title
746.44   TT770

ISBN 0 7207 1755 8

CONTENTS

C.M.PEAR
1988

PART 3
THREADS, EQUIPMENT AND TECHNIQUES

ACKNOWLEDGEMENTS

The author would like to thank the following contributors:

Rob Cox for the photographs on pages 1, 8, 13, 14/15, 16, 17, 19, 20, 21, 22, 23, 24, 25, 27, 28, 29, 30, 38, 39, 40, 41, 42, 43, 44, 45, 46, 48, 49, 50, 51, 52, 55, 58, 59, 62, 65, 66, 67, 69, 70, 73, 74, 77, 78, 79, 80, 84, 87, 91, 92, 93, 94, 95, 97, 99, 101, 106, 107, 110, 111, 113, 116, 118, 199, 123, 124, 125, 129, 130, 137, 138, 140, 141, 142, 143, 145, 146, 156, 157, 160, 161, 162, 163, 168/9, 171, 179; John Hunnex for kindly loaning the photographs on pages 2, 3, 31, 81, 83, 164 and 165; Marilyn Garrow of the Oriental Department, Liberty, London for the embroidered fragment on page 8; the Tate Gallery, London for permission to reproduce the paintings on pages 10 and 36 (page 10, 'Supernovae' © D.A.C.S. 1987); Peter Collingwood for kind permission to feature his woven hanging on page 11; David Prior for the photograph on page 18; Hayward and Martin for the line drawings on pages 22, 26 (right), 39 (right), 40, 41 (left), 44 (right), 54, 62, 63, 64, 67 (bottom), 68, 71, 72, 76, 82, 86 (bottom), 88, 100, 103, 104, 105, 112, 118 (right), 126, 127, 144, 172, 173, 175, 176, 177, 178, 180; Patricia Wright for working the veil on page 23 and Katy Eaton, the model; Sunday Times Syndication Department for the photographs on page 35 (right); embroidered panel on page 37 from the collection of Mrs Caro, London; Elaine Moss for working the pocket and garment on page 43; Hilda Ibrahim for working the embroidery on page 50; the Ruskin Gallery, Collection of the Guild of St George, Sheffield for loan of the photograph on page 60; Nicole Gaulier for kind permission to reproduce her composition on page 61; Freda Wright for working the embroidery on page 70; Sally Mayhew for working the embroidery on page 74; Kjell Sandved for the micro photo on page 75; Martin Durrant for the photographs on pages 90, 137, 152, 153, 154, 155; Michael Fogden/ Bruce Coleman Ltd for the photograph on page 98; Peter Hutchings for the photographs on pages 102, 128, 134/5; Carla Codara for working the patchwork waistcoat featured on page 110 and for assistance with the doll on page 130; Daphne Vizard for working the patchwork and Irene Hall for the knitting on page 116.

INTRODUCTION

Design is a word variously used, but for most of us it would be very easy to agree that to design is to initiate. It is not copying something that has been done before and adding a few changes: to design is to make decisions that are original and, for the artist, visual.

This book is about some of the basic options from which the component parts of a design may be selected or rejected. The designs illustrated are all objects of art rather than industry; some are purely for contemplation and others for practical use.

But whether an artifact is useful or not, whether it represents something or not, the designer must be aware of the basic concepts necessary to form a visually satisfactory end result. Every picture or object gains from having been assembled with some knowledge of visual grammar and composition.

Part 1 of *Design for Embroidery* explores and explains these basic concepts. Part 2 seeks to demonstrate their applications on a larger scale, using more advanced techniques. But whether the design is for a greetings card or a wall panel, the final expression is in the use of needle and thread.

Note: Both metric and imperial measurements are given, but it is better to follow one system or the other, since the measurements are often given in round terms, not the exact equivalent. The commonly used English names for materials have been given throughout but American equivalents are given here:

Black sugar paper: construction paper
Bondaweb: Teflon sheet combined with fusible webbing
Cartridge paper: sketch or drawing paper
Cotton cheesecloth: 100% coarse cotton gauze
Drawing pins: thumb tacks
French chalk: dressmaker's chalk
Vilene: Pelon (or non-woven interfacing)

PART 1
CONCEPTS

SECTION 1: SHAPE

GEOMETRIC VERSUS ORGANIC SHAPE

Shapes are so varied as to be almost limitless. Within this vastness there is perhaps one division: on the one hand there is soft organic shape and on the other hand, angular shape; the first offers gentle undulating edges and the second is characterized by hard, straight-edged confines.

Shape is always two-dimensional. It is helpful simply to think of shape as a silhouette, more often than not so simple that it can be cut out with a pair of scissors.

Shapes of both types are about us everywhere and can be extracted from almost any observed subject.

Daisies *and* Staircase *by John Hunnex.*
These two subjects are in direct contrast – the
daisies show soft, undulating, organic silhouettes
while the staircase illustrates examples of hard,
angular shapes.

SIMPLE PAPER SHAPES

To understand shape at its most basic, it is often useful as a first stage to cut some simple shapes from paper whilst trying hard to keep to one group or the other.

Materials
Black sugar paper
White cartridge paper
Scissors or craft knife
Glue or paste
Odd strips of paper

Method
Taking first the organic group of shapes:
1 Using a pair of scissors or a craft knife, cut from the black paper a selection of shapes with rounded edges.
2 Select a few of these and place them at random on a sheet of white paper.
3 Next, move them around and observe carefully the white shapes emerging from between the black ones. The black shapes could also be arranged in such a way that they touch or overlap one another to produce greater variety and complexity of shape, both in the black and the white.

4 The shapes left behind – the 'background' – will in some ways reiterate the shapes of the cut paper. At this stage you will need to concentrate hard to fully appreciate the relationship of the black shapes to the white spaces.
5 When satisfied, glue into place.
6 Now take four odd strips of paper. Position these in such a way as to 'frame' some of the cut shapes. This selection of an area of the image will determine the character and proportion of the final work. Framing could take the overall shape of a rectangle, square, circle or could be irregular; there could even be more than one part of the image singled out for a closer look. This approach allows greater choice and flexibility, heightens general perception and encourages one to consider a number of options before making a final decision.

This simple procedure also resolves the final confines of all the incomplete shapes at the perimeter. Most important of all, the shape of the motif is now related to the area in which it sits.

Steps 1–5.

In a successful exercise it will be impossible to tell at a distance whether the black paper was stuck to the white paper or the other way round. The reason being that the so-called 'background' no longer exists, but is instead an integral and necessary part of the design as a whole.

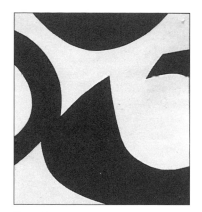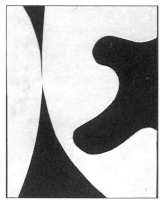

Step 6.

Steps 7–9.

7 Now try using geometric, straight-edged shapes. These do not always have to be placed within a conventional square or rectangle: try starting with a piece of white paper that is already cut into a triangle.

8 Then, make a series of geometric cuts into the triangle and either remove or bend back a few shapes.

9 Continue to experiment with a series of paper triangles.

10 Try removing round-edged organic shapes instead of geometric ones. It is easy to see that the balance of rounded shapes with the triangular whole feels comfortable: for, in spite of the lack of similarity of group, the position of the round shapes on the triangular axis implies a strong visual stability.

Step 10.

THE REPRESENTATIONAL SHAPE

After working with shapes that are purely abstract, that is shapes that do not represent anything, try using shapes that are particular and descriptive: for example, a pair of scissors.

This subject is particularly interesting, since scissors comprise both organic and geometric families of shape and, in addition, their total character is that of a triangle.

There are, of course, many different kinds of scissors and hence many different choices of shape. But even identical scissors given to a group of people to look at and then create an image will not produce the same visual result.

COMPLEX PAPER SHAPES

Materials
A visually interesting pair of scissors
Black sugar paper
White cartridge paper
Scissors for cutting paper
Glue or paste
Odd strips of paper

Method
1 Cut the shape of a pair of scissors from a triangular piece of paper. The triangle should bear some resemblance to the overall character and proportion of the chosen pair of scissors. If possible, look at more than one pair so that different images emerge.
2 Another way would be to cut a series of scissors and then frame or mask with paper strips (as in Step 6 of Simple Paper Shapes on page 4).

The shapes left behind are as important as the shapes which actually describe the scissors. The placing of the motif is not ultimately arbitrary, but instead creates non-descriptive shapes which relate to each other, to the subject and to the whole.

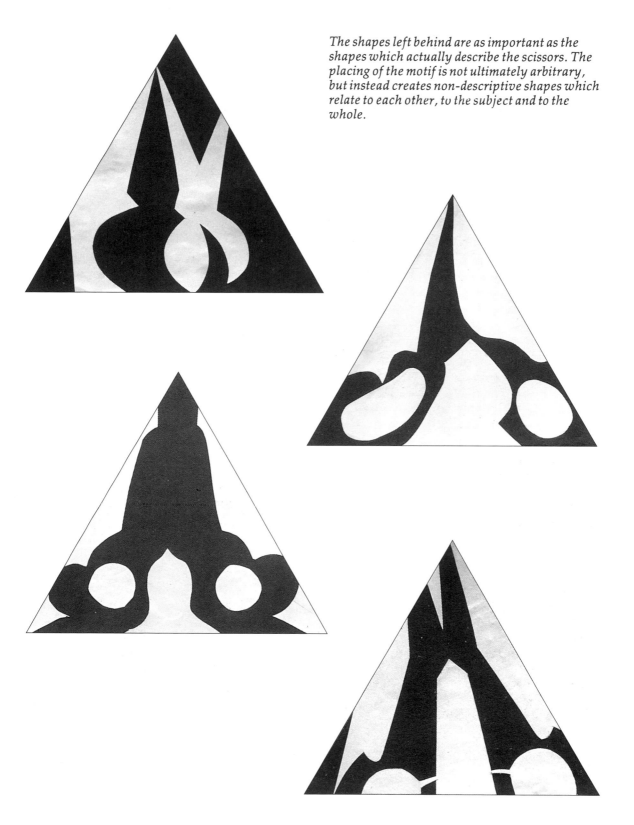

SHAPE IN ART AND APPLIED ART

A positive/negative balance in the distribution of shapes is a fundamental of all art. Examples can be found in many works of art; indeed it has its origins centuries ago in China. It is known there as Yin Yang or T'ai Chi and represents balanced strengths equating to female/male, passive/active, respectively. Fine extant examples can, for instance, be seen on the embroidered Dragon Robes displayed in the Victoria and Albert Museum, London.

The Yin Yang symbol consists of two undecorated shapes, originally one black and one white, of equal size, organically dividing a circle by means of a reverse image. The two abut and

Yin Yang symbol on silk mat (Liberty of London).

Basic Yin Yang symbol.

recede, form a positive and a negative which together make a whole. Neither shape is more important than the other, and both are required to form a complement, one to the other.

It is this total interaction and dependence one upon the other which is so aptly expressed in a poem thought to have been written by the Chinese poet Lao Tse some two thousand years ago:

> We put thirty spokes together and call it a wheel;
> But it is on the space that there is nothing that the utility
>   of the wheel depends.
> We turn clay to make a vessel;
> But it is on the space where there is nothing that the
>   utility of the vessel depends.
> We pierce doors and windows to make a house; and it is
>   on these spaces where there is nothing that the
>   utility of the house depends.
> Therefore, just as we take advantage of what is, we
>   should recognise the utility of what is not.

from *The Way and its Power* translated by Arthur Waley

In Japan this symbol is known as In Yo. The use of balanced space is a dominant feature of all Japanese art. A simple yet satisfactory example is the gold laid work embroidery on a silk fan illustrated here.

Contemporary Japanese embroidery still follows the ancient principles of design.

Painters, too, have been drawn to strengths of a binary nature. Bridget Riley (b. 1931) and Victor Vasarély (b. 1908), both working in the 1950s and 1960s, produced numerous series of work in which movement was created by means of abutting and receding geometric shape.

Supernovae by Victor Vasarély.

Microgauze *by Peter Collingwood.*
Black linen with steel rods. Peter
Collingwood, the British weaver, is well
known for his emphasis on spaces. His
world famous black and white hangings
clearly depend on the reciprocal dark/
light or negative/positive principle.

11

SHAPE IN NATURE

Soon you will instinctively see shape in everything, and particularly in the natural world.

The small beech leaf illustrated is in the early stages of disintegration. The series of small holes cannot be clearly described as either circles or squares or rectangles; instead, more accurately, they could be called square-rounds or rounded rectangles. Note, too, that the shapes in which these little spaces rest, in other words the spaces between the veins, are all 'softened' rectangles. Thus visually, the leaf and its decayed area are responding one to another in order to achieve harmony. Nature has so perfectly resolved for us a difficult design problem: that of combining hard and soft shapes.

Beech leaf.

SHAPE WITH EQUAL TONES

There are many ways to record, on paper, shapes that one has seen. One of the simplest of these is to use paint of only one colour, or even simpler, no colour at all, i.e. black, white or greys. In this illustration white has been used. Try applying the paint with the simplest of tools: a sponge. This method is so easy and pleasurable that any anxiety a beginner may be feeling will quickly disappear.

Painting, in this instance, is merely an aid and a method of setting down, as fast as possible, the shapes one sees.

Choose a subject that is likely to be around, or near you, for a number of days so that it can be looked at on many occasions and perhaps be used for repeated painting sessions. The trials of this painting method eventually led to the design illustrated here which has been based on a patch of nasturtium flowers.

Materials
Paper: something with a bit of colour (e.g. brown parcel paper, large old brown envelopes or coloured art paper)
Paint (e.g. white water-based: anything from decorator's emulsion to white ink or a tube of designers gouache)
Bowl of water
Small cube of fine sponge
Odd scraps of paper on which to mix paint
Tracing paper
Pencil

Method
1 Start by enjoying the sponge and the paint.

Put a nice blob of paint on to an odd scrap of paper. Thoroughly dampen and squeeze out the sponge whilst the hand is in the water. Now rub the sponge in the paint until some of the different consistencies are experienced. This will allow the wetness or dryness of the mix to be appreciated. The traditional method of mixing paint on a conventional palette containing many rather deep pans can produce a series of mini swimming pools of quite the wrong colour and inappropriate consistency – a waste of both paint and time.

2 Now make marks of any kind on the paper. Sometimes press, sometimes lightly drag the sponge across the surface. Try all the contrasts of a thickly-loaded sponge to one thinly filled. Squeeze the sponge into a small shape or use it on its edge.

If you prefer, a 5cm (2in) decorator's brush or paint pad could be used instead of a sponge: both allow the beginner to forget the traditional tools of the artist and, in turn, the traditional styles of representation. With a sponge there is nothing to emulate and therefore nothing can possibly go wrong! The fears many beginners have of painting will vanish as elegant and beautiful marks appear.

3 When you are used to using the sponge, try producing a simple representation of an actual subject:

4 If the painting is to be used for a design, it is helpful if a pencil outline is applied to the selected shapes to define them more clearly for the next step – tracing.

5 Trace. This should not be a copy of every detail but a considered extraction of both painted and non-painted shapes.

Step 4.

6 Using an odd piece of paper, mark and cut out a hole in the centre about 25cm (10in) in diameter (about the size of an average dinner plate).

7 Place this circle over the traced shapes, moving it around until a balance of positive and negative shapes begins to emerge.

8 Mark the position of this circle on the tracing. Cut out the tracing on this circular line.

Step 6.

Step 8.

Step 9.

9 Then cut into the design to give a fretted edge. This gives added interest and breaks the solidity. For example, remove any dark shapes that happen to be at the edge.

These experiments with simple painted shapes can be used as the basis for a design for a wedding veil (see pages 18–23) or net curtains or anything else of a transparent and delicate nature.

WEDDING VEIL

Detail of individual motifs.

Materials

Final tracing from Step 9, page 17

Pencil (not too soft otherwise it will rub off onto the fabric when working on Step 9)

2m (2yd) Bondaweb

2m (2yd) organdie

Assorted transparent fabric pieces or remnants (e.g. silk organza, lace, sheer wetlook, etc; preferably in off-white rather than stark white)

3m (3yd) off-white or cream nylon or silk tulle

4 reels off-white machine embroidery cotton (DMC number 50, 500gm reels in colour 712)

Sharp pointed scissors

Sewing machine with swing needle

Method

1 Turn the traced shape (from Step 9, page 17) over so that the image is reversed.

2 Place a piece of Bondaweb over the whole tracing, smooth side up.

3 Trace the whole motif with a hard pencil.

4 Continue to make enough Bondaweb tracings to scatter over the whole width of the veil (seven were used in the one illustrated).

Steps 5–6.

5 Further smaller motifs will be needed to continue the design: cut a circle of 20cm (8in), or the equivalent of a dessert plate, and a 15cm (6in) circle, or the equivalent of a side plate, out of odd paper. Use these circular 'masks' or 'windows' to look for two further motifs from your earlier paintings.

6 Place this circle over the traced painting, moving it around until a balance of positive and negative shapes begins to emerge.

7 Mark the position of this circle on the tracing. Cut out the tracing on this circular line.

Step 8.

Steps 5–6.

8 Then cut into the design to give a fretted edge. This gives added interest and breaks the solidity. For example, remove any dark shapes that happen to be at the edge.
9 Follow the same procedure as described in 1–4 above. A greater number of motifs in the smaller sizes may be necessary. In the veil illustrated eight medium-size and ten small were found to be about right.
10 Working on your Bondaweb tracings, proceed as follows.
11 Using sharp scissors, remove one shape from one Bondaweb tracing.

Step 8.

Steps 12–13.

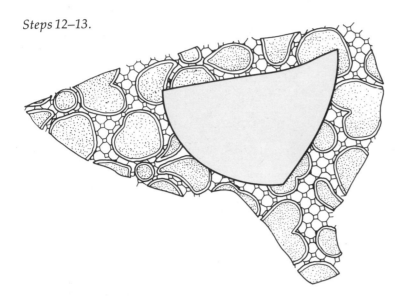

RIGHT: *Veil showing delicate effect of applied shapes. Nylon tulle falls softly – silk tulle falls even more finely, but it is about ten times more expensive.*

12 Place this small shape, glue-side down, onto the *back* of the fabric to be applied.

13 Iron on. With transparent or very thin fabrics it is advisable to place a clean sheet of paper or spare Bondaweb backing paper on the ironing board, otherwise the glue will penetrate through to the cover. Place a second piece of Bondaweb backing paper on *top* of the fabric to be applied to prevent making marks on the pale fabric.

14 Following the paper edge exactly, cut out.

15 Remove the paper backing from the shape.

16 Place a piece of organdie – large enough to carry the whole motif – onto the ironing board.

17 Lay the complete Bondaweb tracing, glue-side (rough) uppermost, on the organdie. Secure at the top with two pins. This now determines exactly where on the organdie to place the newly prepared shape for application. Place prepared shape through Bondaweb hole – somewhat like filling in the next piece of a jigsaw.

18 Iron the shape into place.

19 Continue in this way until all the shapes have been applied.

20 Finally, secure each shape with zig-zag stitches on the sewing machine. The stitch length and width will depend on the fabric to be applied: for the veil illustrated, a Bernina machine was set with a stitch width of 1½ and a stitch length of almost zero for all the different types of fabric used. If the machine spool-case is one that has a small additional threader hole in the horn, it is a good idea to thread the bottom cotton through this before bringing the cotton to the top. The result is a far more compact zig-zag stitch.

21 When all the motifs are complete, trim the spare organdie away, taking care not to snip any machine stitching. Also consider cutting away a few internal shapes: the design may benefit from this additional tone.

Position of machine needle for zig-zag stitching.

22 Arrange the shapes around the veil. Pin. Attach by hand with careful slip stitching.

SHAPE IN RELATIONSHIP TO COLOUR

When using coloured shapes, particularly if they are to be transposed to fabric, a greater number and variety may be necessary to create sufficient interest and challenge.

It can be very satisfying developing a subject or theme for some length of time. A great deal of confidence can be gained by continuing to look at and to draw or to paint the same thing in many different ways (e.g. not just the same species of plant, but the same plant), time and time again, in different lights and from different view-points.

PRIMROSE APPLIQUÉ

Simple painting of primroses made by sponge method (Steps 1–2, page 26).

Materials

A subject – such as potted primroses

Plain paper (preferably white and of a reasonable quality; cheap paper tends to absorb coloured paint and gives disappointing results)

Water-based paints (any kind will do, but the easiest to use are those in tubes rather than in pots or hard blocks; designers gouache is very pleasing and easy to use)

Small bowl of water

A small cube of sponge to mix and apply the paint (alternatively, a 2.5cm (1in) decorator's brush or pad gives equally satisfying broad and simple marks)

Tracing paper

Materials continued
Pencil
Bondaweb (a large enough piece to cover the whole motif to be worked)
Fabric or heavy sew-in Vilene (large enough to become the ground area with an extra 5cm (2in) all round for turning)
Assortment of small fabric pieces suitable for appliqué (i.e. not too large or open a grain or weave)
Machine embroidery cotton number 50 (use colours that are a near match to the fabrics to be applied unless a contrast is wanted; ordinary sewing cotton could be used, but it is thicker and therefore a little more prominent when worked)
Sharp pointed scissors
Sewing machine with a swing needle

Method
1 Make a *simple* painting by the sponge method; make several paintings, if possible, and then make a choice. Leave out all very fine detail depicting intricate lines or textures: aim to depict only *shapes* in lovely colours.
2 Select a portion of the work by masking off with strips of paper the area not required.

3 Trace selectively, including only the minimum number of lines. These lines merely serve to denote boundaries between one colour and another. Whilst tracing, be aware of all the positive and reciprocal negative shapes.

Sometimes it is necessary to make a series of tracings, one after the other, to simplify the statement. It is therefore better to trace from the last tracing rather than from the initial one.
4 Turn the final tracing over, with the wrong side facing.
5 Place a layer of Bondaweb on top of this reversed tracing. There is only one side on which one can comfortably draw and that should naturally be uppermost. Trace again. This forms the master pattern from which all the shapes will be cut.
6 Mark every Bondaweb shape with a vertical arrow.
7 With sharp scissors, remove one shape from the Bondaweb.
8 Place this small shape, glue-side down, onto the *back* of the fabric to be applied. It is helpful to the finished result to place the arrow on the vertical grain of the fabric.
9 Iron on.
10 Carefully and accurately cut out the fabric following the paper edge.
11 Remove paper backing from this shape.
12 Place ground fabric on the table. Lay the whole Bondaweb tracing, rough (i.e.

Step 3.

Steps 7–9.

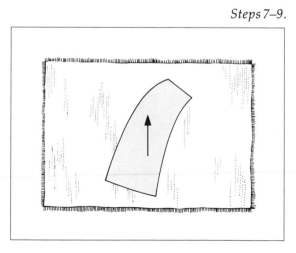

26

Step 15.

glue-side) uppermost, one shape re-moved in the correct position on the ground fabric. This will determine the exact position of the newly prepared fab-ric shape.

13 Iron shape into place.

14 Proceed in this way until several neighbouring shapes are fixed to the ground fabric.

15 Secure by sewing around each shape with a zig-zag stitch on the sewing machine. The stitch length and width will depend on the fabric to be applied. (The example shown is in Dupion fabric, ap-plied with a stitch width of number 2 and a stitch length of virtually zero on a Ber-nina machine.)

16 When preparing to sew, the machine needle should be positioned so that it swings from the edge of the fabric in-wards (see illustration on page 22). The smoothest results and effects are gained from applying fabrics that are of equal weight (i.e. all of velvet, all of Viyella, etc.) but some of the richest surfaces are achieved by using a mixture!

The painting of a dish of primroses (Step 1).

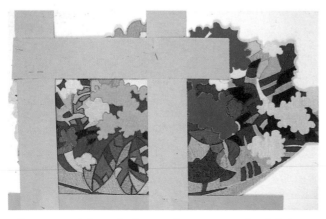

All or some of the painting can be transposed to fabric.

The dish of primroses *(above)* develops the same theme, but is a slightly more complicated painting. It has still been done mostly with a sponge, but is composed of a richer group of coloured shapes. The same steps were followed as for the primrose appliqué.

Selected detail of appliqué.

SECTION 2: LINE

Line is a concept of great contrasts. It can be thick or thin, long or short, straight or curved, dark or light, solid or broken, rough or smooth, shiny or matt, flat or in relief, closely placed one to another or widely set apart. It can be found in almost everything we look at, both man-made and natural.

These few examples show its diversity:

LEFT: *Few lines could appear simpler than this one painted by the contemporary Japanese shodo artist Tokei Akagi in this piece* Wa, *which symbolises the spirited cry of self-confidence and strength.*

BELOW: Blades of Grass *by John Hunnex. Simple, too, are the blades of grass reflected in water in this striking photograph.*

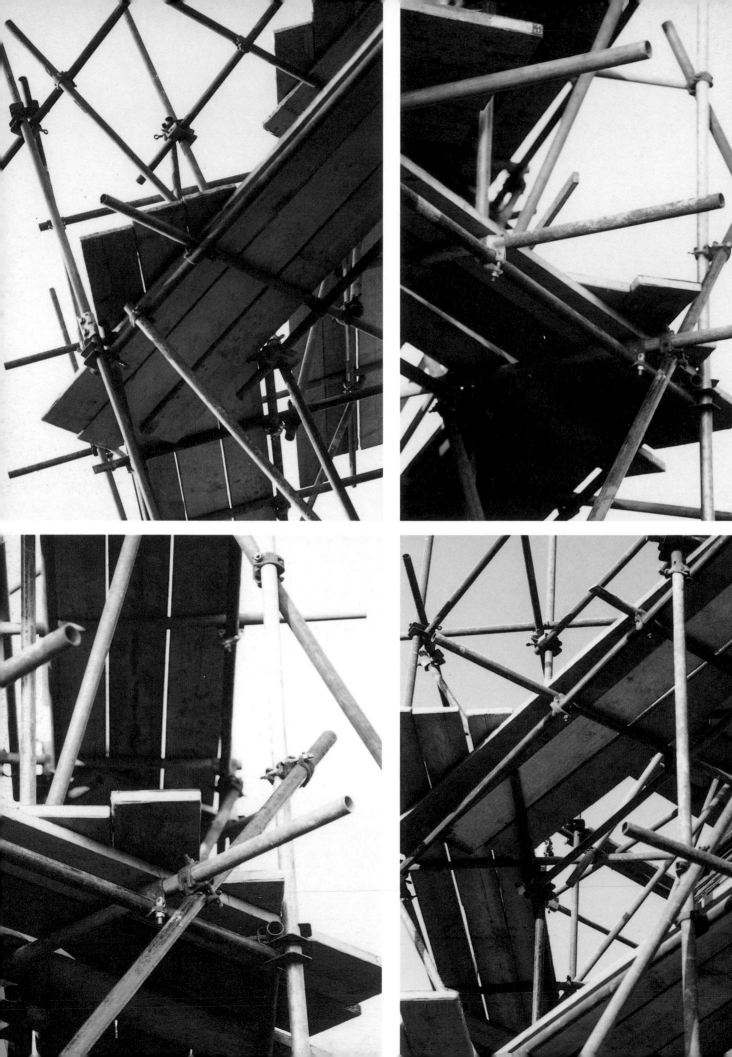

LEFT: *Scaffolding in England.*
Scaffolding and scaffolding boards provide lines
of a different character: unequal widths of line
are made more interesting by the lines of light
between the timbers.

THIS PAGE: *Scaffolding in China.*
Compare the British and Chinese structures. The
first are lines of strength whilst the second have
more in common with the delicacy of lace.

Train your eye to perceive and appreciate line in as many situations as possible and you will become aware of its many design possibilities. Keep a scrapbook of sketches and photographs to remind you of what you have seen.

Certain subjects are an inspiration for raised and sculptural work. For example, magnificent high-relief lines can be interpreted from the many ceramic roof tiles that clad the Dragon Gate in the western hills of Yunnan, China.

Lines of quite a different character, beautifully corded, twisted, knotted and divided, are expressed in braided African hair styles.

Meryon *by Franz Kline (1910–1962).*
Many paintings are totally dependent upon line;
in some American Abstract Expressionist
examples, the line is used not to represent
something but as a statement in its own right. The
gestural painted marks of Franz Kline are not
unlike calligraphy. Each is a beautiful statement
simply about line.

For many artists and craftsmen line *is* the content, the medium used *is* the message. This is particularly so in calligraphy and abstract painting. It is rewarding to compare the different line techniques of old masters: for example, compare the minimal line of Ingres with the gestural line of Rubens.

White Line (1972). Embroidered wall panel by the author.
Statements in line can easily be expressed with threads. Threads very naturally extend the range of media that are capable of producing line.

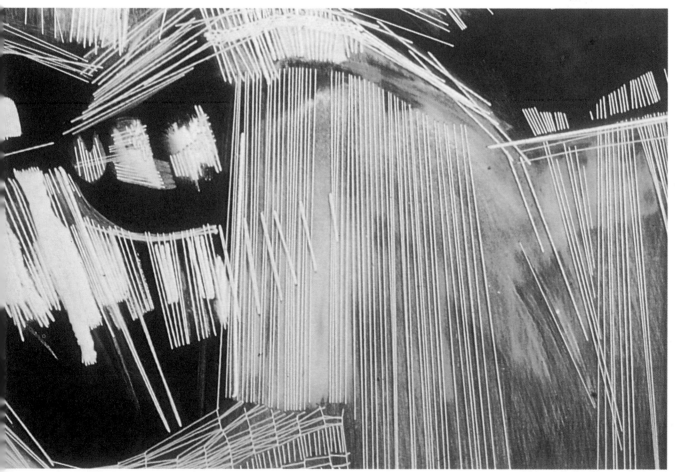

A PAINTING EXERCISE

It is important to recognise the value of a simple visual statement, particularly when it is expressed by minimal means.

Line at its simplest can be a mark on paper made with pencil, pen or brush. It can also be made with a sponge. By using a sponge you will again avoid any temptation to relate your work to traditional methods of classical drawing and painting or to any traditional styles of representation.

This exercise may seem over simple initially, but anyone who tries it for the first time will soon become aware that the more you practise the more subtle and varied are the lines achieved.

Steps 1–2.

Materials
Black paint or ink
Several sheets of white paper (the quality can be inferior)
Water in a suitable container (large enough to put the hand in when rinsing the sponge)
Cube of sponge about 5cm (2in)
Odd strips of paper

Method
1 Make all kinds of mark on the paper with the ink or paint-loaded sponge. Experiment with the sponge when it is rather dry and also when it is very wet.
2 In the early stages it is advisable to keep to black alone and so avoid any confusion or complexity created by coloured lines. Experiment with the paint mixed thickly and thinly (as for a delicate watercolour wash).

Different results can also be obtained just by varying the pressure put upon the sponge – pressing down heavily or hardly touching the paper at all. An exciting variety of contrasts will gradually evolve – lines that vary from wide to narrow, broken to solid, heavy to light, etc. Continue experimenting until you have several pages from which to select an area of greatest contrast.

SAMPLER

This sampler shows a simple transposition from paint to thread.

Materials

Good quality tracing paper (greaseproof paper is not suitable as it is too soft for use in the transposition of the design to cloth by the 'prick and pounce' method)

Pencil

Ruler

Assortment of crewel needles

Pins

French chalk or talcum powder

Small pad of felt, or similar, for use with the chalk

Small paint brush (number 1 sable is best)

Water-based white paint

Tacking cotton

Ground fabric (preferably white)

Rectangular embroidery frame (large enough to carry the whole work)

Threads. DMC perlé number 5: one skein in black. Stranded cotton: one skein in black. Laine tapisserie: one skein or oddment of knitting wool in black

Staples or drawing pins

Scissors

Odd strips of paper

Method

1 Using four strips of paper, mask or frame an area from your pages of painted lines already made *(opposite)*. These should include a balance of black lines to white space, and in addition include a variety of types of line within the mark itself.

2 Trace this piece, but select only the main divisions that separate the major changes within the rectangle.

Step 1.

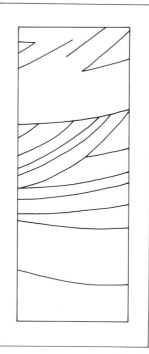

Step 2.

3 Turn the tracing over and with a large crewel needle poke holes on all the traced lines about 5mm (¼in) apart. In this way, the needle will *enter the wrong side of the drawing* which gives the right side of the tracing a rough texture not unlike a cheese grater.

4 Lay this, with the rough texture of the tracing uppermost, on the right side of the piece of fabric.

5 Holding the tracing paper down firmly with one hand, take a small pad of felt in the other hand. Dab the felt into the French chalk and rub it gently and systematically through the holes using a gentle circular movement.

6 Carefully remove the tracing paper. Rows of powder dots should now be visible.

7 Join these by using a fine paint brush and a water-based white paint. You will need to make many tiny strokes as the brush inevitably collects powder.

8 Tack all round the painted lines so you have a line which follows the rectangle of the design.

Step 5.

9 Sharply shake the fabric to remove any excess powder.

10 Place fabric on a rectangular embroidery frame using staples, drawing pins or conventional lacing, depending on the frame used (see pages 172–3). If the fabric is too small or too delicate to go directly onto a frame, tack it to a larger piece of backing material, e.g. a soft cotton fabric.

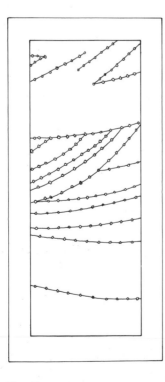

Step 3.

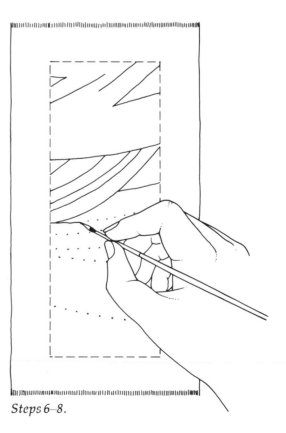

Steps 6–8.

11 Now transpose to stitchery. Only those stitches that will give a linear effect should be considered, e.g. running stitch, whipped chain stitch and twisted chain stitch. These stitches are also successful when massed together to fill an area.

It is better to select only a few stitches: simplicity usually leads to a richer end result. Select those stitches that will express the main contrasts. Too many and the work becomes a sampler of every known treatment of the embroidered line!

Thread should also be selected with care according to the scale of the work in hand, e.g. rug wool on a finely woven cloth would be very difficult to sew. The most versatile threads are stranded cotton, perlé cotton in all the weights of 3, 5 and 8 (thick, medium and fine), retors à broder, laine tapisserie, broder Medicis and crewel wool. There are, of course, many other interesting and suitable threads including those used for crochet, knitting and weaving.

12 Continue to embroider in simple lines trying hard to reproduce the character of the original painted lines, i.e. solid, broken, thick, thin, etc.

13 Stretch the finished piece (see page 176).

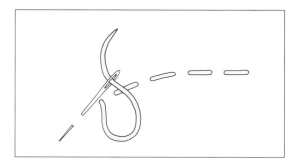

Running stitch.

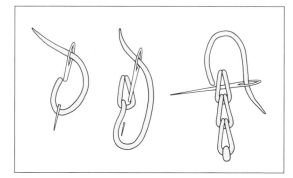

Whipped chain stitch.

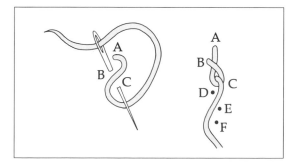

Twisted chain stitch.

The embroidery recreates the character of the original painted lines.

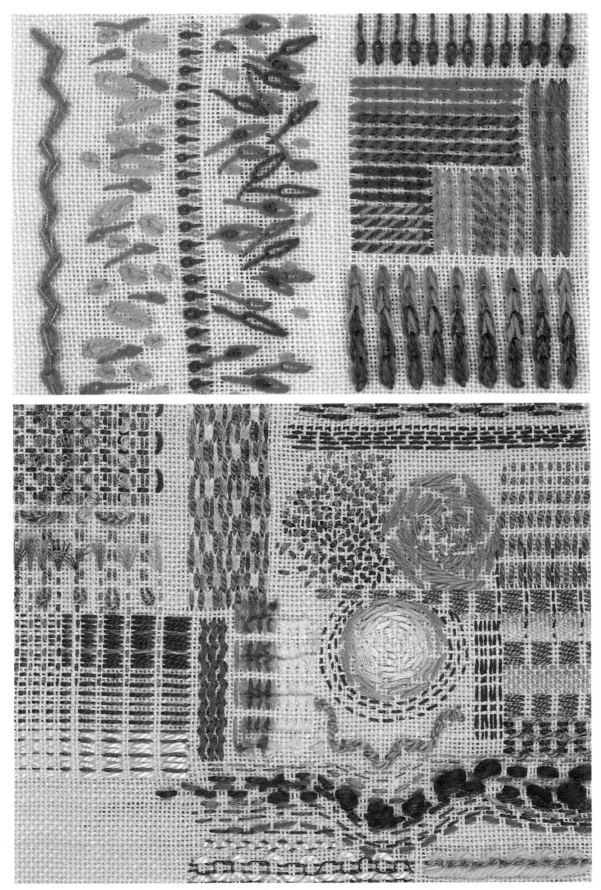

These samplers show the potential diversity of chain stitch and running stitch.

EMBROIDERED POCKETS

The simple approach of the sampler (page 39) can be applied to a useful article for practical, everyday use. This example is a pocket on a dress, but the technique can be applied to almost any household article from bedcovers to curtains, from table linen to chair coverings.

Simple stitchery, of the correct weight and well positioned, can become a striking decorative feature on a garment.

Materials
Black paint or ink
Several sheets of white paper (the quality can be inferior)
Water in a suitable container (large enough to put the hand in when rinsing the sponge)
Cube of sponge about 5cm (2in)
Odd strips of paper
Good quality tracing paper
Pencil
Ruler
Assortment of crewel needles
Pins
French chalk or talcum powder
Small pad of felt, or similar, for use with the chalk
Small paint brush (number 1 sable is best)
Water-based white paint
Tacking cotton
Rectangular embroidery frame (large enough to carry the whole work)
4m (4⅓yd) fabric, for example cotton cheesecloth
Style pattern no. 4383, or any personal choice of pattern
Threads. DMC retors à broder: 2 skeins of black. Perlé number 5: 4 skeins of black. Stranded cotton: 1 skein of black. Coton à broder: 1 skein of black.
Staples or drawing pins
Scissors
Odd strips of paper

Method
1 Produce a few pages of sponge marks as described on page 38.

2 Lay one of the pocket pattern pieces onto a larger sheet of paper (any cheap paper will do). Mark on it the *finished* shape of the pocket.
3 Cut out this shape from the sheet of paper. It will now be like a pocket-shaped 'frame'.
4 Place it on top of the black line paintings. Move this frame or window all over the different sheets of black painted marks to select the area that will produce the most well-balanced motif for the pocket.
5 Attach this window mount in position on the painting, with either pins or glue. This will be the final image for transposition to stitchery.
6 Trace. Use only the lines that define distinct changes within the motif and above all keep it simple.
7 Turn this tracing over and trace the tracing to reverse the image for the second pocket.
8 Taking each of the tracings in turn, one

Step 6.   *Step 7.*

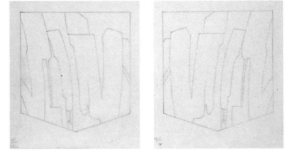

Steps 4–5.

Step 8.

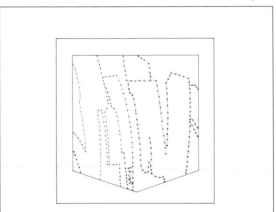

for the right side pocket and one for the left, poke small holes about 5mm (¼in) apart, from the *wrong side of the image to the right side*.

9 Study the cutting layout on the dress pattern instruction sheet.

Step 11.

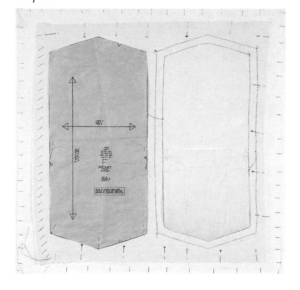

10 Cut from the length of fabric the required amount for *both* pockets. Allow at least double the recommended turnings but do not cut out either pocket: keep the fabric in one piece.

11 Place the pattern piece for the pocket on the fabric with the straight grain of the fabric corresponding to the vertical arrow on the pattern. Tack around the shape.

12 Tack another line 15mm (⅝in) inside the shape to denote the eventual sewing line.

13 Place each prepared tracing in position within the appropriate half of the tacked area.

14 Follow the method described on page 40, Steps 3–9.

15 Transpose to stitchery (as described on page 41). Continue to embroider in simple lines trying to reproduce the character of the original painted marks. Remember to reverse the embroidery for the second pocket.

16 Stretch the finished embroidery (see page 176).

17 Make up the garment and apply the pockets as instructed in the pattern notes.

Completed pocket.

SIMPLE GREETINGS CARD

As skills with paint, sponge or brush increase, it becomes very easy to produce simple representational images. These images, if done on heavy paper, can then directly support simple line stitchery.

Materials

White paint (anything from decorator's emulsion to designers gouache)

Bowl of water

Paint brush; a good quality one does produce better results. (Try a number 4 sable hair)

A larger brush or a cube of sponge (necessary if wider marks are wanted)

Paper (thick and preferably in a dark colour)

Card (thin and lightweight for making into the actual folding mount)

A piece of spare cartridge (drawing) paper large enough to line the back of the mounted work

Craft knife for cutting the window mount

Glue or paste

Assorted crewel needles

Assorted oddments of white threads of different thicknesses. In the example shown, DMC perlé cotton, stranded cotton and coton à broder have been used.

Method

1 Observe any object, such as a plant. Very simply, put down just the outline of the shapes. Vary the amount of paint on the brush and the pressure put upon the brush whilst working.

2 Continue until you have a whole sheet of paper covered with drawings of great contrast and variety where the brush has been allowed to move freely about the paper.

3 Select the most successful area both in terms of size for the project envisaged, and for the simplest contrasts of line (as seen in the illustration).

4 Start the embroidery directly onto the sketch. It is a good idea (and often visually more satisfactory) to use only straight stitches of varying lengths and widths. The stitchery should be used as an additional dimension to complement the initial statement in paint. As the finished example shows, painted lines are joined by thread lines which may be shiny, matt, rough, etc.

5 Cut a card mount (see page 179).

LEFT: *Steps 1–2.*

BELOW: *White gouache lines painted on black sugar paper provide a basis on which to sew. Such a painting has many uses: here it has been used to make a unique greetings card (Steps 3–4).*

RIGHT: *A further stage could be to try a coloured painting superimposed with embroidery.*

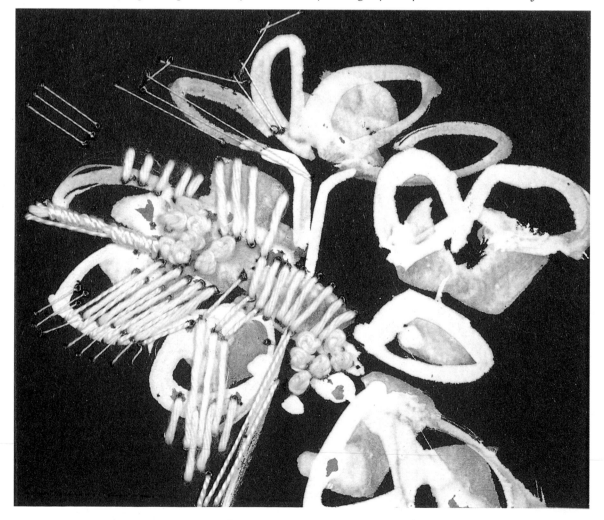

STOOL-TOP CUSHION

This cushion has been designed to illustrate the range of possibilities available when using line with colour and is in contrast to previous projects which have dealt only with the possibilities of black and white.

The cushion is dependent on a more complicated painting but still one that uses the sponge. These initial broad areas of colour (made by sponge) form the basis for additional, easy methods of achieving the all-over linear treatment illustrated. One of these methods has been accomplished by tying together several different sizes of paint brushes; a cluster of lines can be produced with only one movement of the hand, and there are many more experiments you could try.

Stool-top cushion. The cushion has been made up as a slim pad and trimmed with a twisted cord of Medici wool (see page 180). The painting opposite was instrumental in directing the colour of every line, its position, length and frequency.

Original painting. Coloured lines can go in many directions as this painting shows. Thus simple observation of an ordinary subject can be developed to become a richly decorated cushion.

The painting contains a multitude of colours so there is a lot to think about when it comes to transposing the design sheet to stitchery. But only one stitch and one type of thread have been chosen. This simplification allows every effort to be concentrated on the *colour* of the line rather than on the different kinds of textures or types of line.

The whole work can be seen as a massing together of lines to create an overall activation of surface. By the time the final choice of the area of the painting to be used for the design is made, there is no evidence of a formal composition or focal point, or indeed any trace of an original motif. In this case the fundamental inspiration was a crab apple tree in full fruit, but during the process of selection and transposition the original source has become less obvious.

Materials

A suitable painting (one with an obvious linear quality)
Tracing paper of the best quality
Pencil
Ruler
Selection of crewel needles
French chalk or talcum powder
Fine paint brush
White water-based paint
Felt pad
Threads. DMC Medici wool in ¼ hanks or 25 metre skeins. The following colours were used for the example illustrated: 101 cherry, 104, 104A, 106 rust to pinks. 120bis, 122, 123, 124, 124bis, 125 wines to pinks. 204, 204bis, 211, 506, 507, 508 warm and cool greys. 175 navy, 412 green, 307, 309 beige to brown
Fabric: 60cm (24in) square. Something strong yet finely and softly woven to allow easy passage of the needle through the cloth. This example is worked on a 60cm (24in) wide tailor's canvas
Rectangular embroidery frame (large enough to carry the whole work)
Drawing pins or staples if a conventional embroidery frame is not available
Scissors

Method

1 Measure the stool top or cushion size required.
2 Make a window in a spare piece of paper to correspond to one quarter of the above dimensions.
3 Using this window seek a suitable area of the painting. It should be one that will look well if repeated. (In this case repeated three times to complete the four quarters of the design).

LEFT: *Final choice of area of painting to transpose to stitchery (Steps 2–3).*

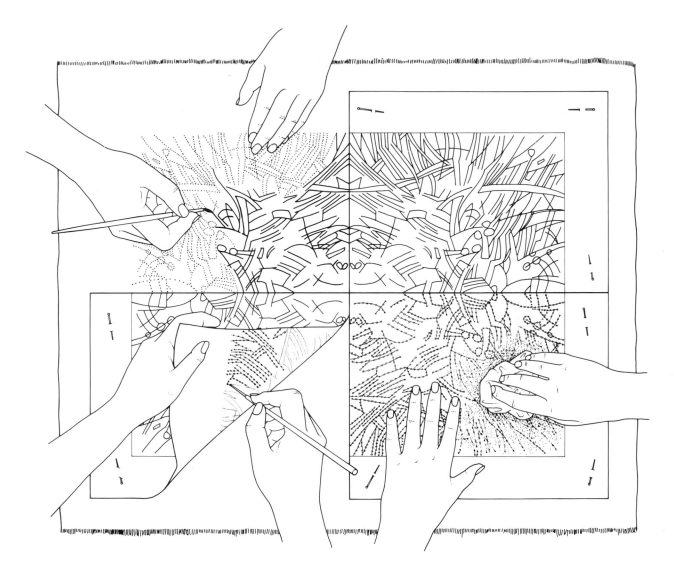

4 Trace. (This will be for the top right of the design.)

5 Turn tracing over and make a tracing of the reverse (for the bottom right).

6 Poke holes in these two tracings (see page 40, (Step 3). Make sure that one tracing is kept as a reverse image.

7 Divide the fabric into four quarters using a tacked line.

8 Take one tracing. Decide which corner is to form part of the centre of the design and place this accordingly (top right or bottom right).

9 Follow the method described on page 40, Steps 3–9.

10 When repeating this tracing note that the position for the repeat will fall in the *diagonal* quarter of the fabric (top left or bottom left).

11 Repeat with the other tracing.

12 Place fabric on a rectangular embroidery frame using staples, drawing pins or conventional lacing, depending on the frame used (see pages 172–3).

13 Now transpose to stitchery. In this example, whipped chain stitch (see page 41) has been used throughout with a double thickness of wool.

Detail of finished embroidery.

SECTION 3: COLOUR

Colour has the potential of being the most powerful or the most subordinate of concepts: it can be vivid and bright or subdued and subtle. It is everywhere in our natural surroundings and in the things we make. Everything about us is coloured in some way.

We all see colour differently. How often do we hear of great dilemmas about whether a colour is really this or that: one's own definition of a particular colour is very different from the assessment of others. Throughout our lives we make colour decisions, some consciously, some unconsciously and intuitively. For example, the way we dress, furnish our homes or plant our gardens is largely a matter of colour.

The more consciously we observe colour in our environment the more we realise its power. Look at the dominance of the blue in the pot of cornflowers sitting in the market in Helsinki. The bunch of flowers takes precedence over everything that surrounds it because of its colour.

Topiary garden at Levens Hall, Cumbria.
The magic grows as one then goes on to realise
that there are so many different blues, all with
power; but power only according to where and
how they are situated in relation to other colours.
Compare the blue of these forget-me-nots with
that of the cornflowers.

Colour is also about deciding which colour goes
with another; not simply in equal amounts but in
what proportion. Look, for example, at the
astonishing feather donated by Wally the parrot
of Denver, USA! Here, very basic colours occupy
well-defined areas: two primary colours (red and
yellow) together with two greens, one of which is
virtually a true green as found on a secondary
colour wheel.

Colour proportions, positions and combinations are not always so straightforward: it is best to start as simply as possible and let complexities grow slowly. There are plenty of books on the theory theory of colour (see Further Reading page 182). These are helpful and important. However, if one can create without the help of theory then, as Johannes Itten wrote in his *Art of Colour* "If you, unknowing, are able to create masterpieces in colour, then unknowledge is your way. But if you are unable to create masterpieces in colour out of your unknowledge, then you ought to look for knowledge".

If you find colour decisions difficult, start simply be observing colour. Use a camera or paints to record what you see. This practical approach will help to capture the subject of interest and can evolve alongside the study of colour theory.

Cyclamen by the author.
This painting was made as a colour note for
future reference.

Observation is the key to understanding colour. John Ruskin (1819–1900), artist and art critic, collected items specifically so that people could be taught to *see*. His collection, housed in the Ruskin Gallery, Sheffield, is the finest example available on 'how to look' and observe.

"The first necessity of beauty in colour is gradation . . .

The second necessity in colour is mystery of subtlety . . .

It is the best possible sign of a colour when nobody who sees it knows what to call it, or how to give an idea of it to anyone else . . .

Nature produces all her loveliest colour in some kind of solid or liquid glass or crystal. The colours of the opal are produced in vitreous flint mixed with water and the loveliest colours ever granted to human sight – those of morning and evening clouds before or after rain – are produced on minute particles of finely divided water, or perhaps, sometimes, ice."

John Ruskin: *Lectures on Art Works*. Library Edition. Vol XX, p 166

Gradually you will be able to make distinctions between colour that is real or 'local' as in the cornflowers, forget-me-nots and parrot feather, and that which is abstract and unrelated to the subject. Many examples of the latter can be found, particularly in paintings of the Fauve period (early twentieth century), such as Matisse's *The Pink Onions,* and in the work of the German Expressionists; *Yellow Horses* by Franz Marc (1880–1916) is particularly well-known.

Colour can also be used in a totally abstract way, that is not as applied to representational imagery but used as the image itself.

LEFT: *Opal from the Ruskin Gallery, Sheffield.*

BELOW: Composition *(1980) by Nicole Gaulier (b. 1939). Hand embroidery in chain stitch using DMC stranded cotton. Colour is used here in a non-representational way.*

EMBROIDERED GREETINGS CARD
(NON-REPRESENTATIONAL)

A helpful first step in the use of colour is to allow the local colour of an observed subject to influence the initial selection of colours to be included. In other words, the resulting artifact will not necessarily be a representation of the shape or form of the thing seen but, instead, will solely depend on the extraction of colours; perhaps even in their original proportion and position. The parrot feather, illustrated on page 58, is a perfect example. It contains only a few colours and yet has a striking beauty. This lies mainly in the size and position of each colour area, both in terms of one colour to another and to the area as a whole.

A simple embroidered pattern, sewn onto card to form a personal greeting. This design stems directly from observation of the parrot feather.

Materials
Piece of thin lightweight 1mm card (white) approximately 20.5 × 10cm (8 × 4in) and of 250–300 microns weight
Thread. DMC perlé cotton number 5: greens 367, 703, lemon 907. Retors à broder number 4: lime green 2218, yellow 2444. Stranded cotton: scarlet 666. One skein of each will obviously make more than one motif
Needle: crewel or tapestry of the same

size as the holes that will be poked in the card
Stiletto or similar tool to poke fine holes in the card
Scissors
Pencil and ruler
A Stanley or craft knife may be necessary if the card needs cutting to a desired size

Method
1 Using a pencil and ruler make a series of lines, both horizontally and vertically at 4mm (⅛in) apart on the card. Use the centre of one half of the card (to allow for the fold).

Steps 1–2.

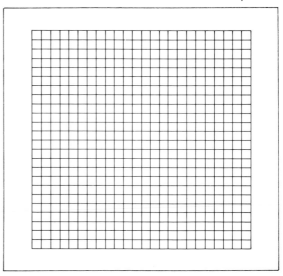

62

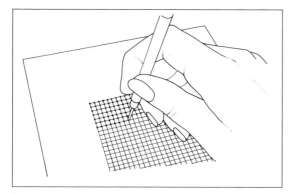

Step 3.

2 In the example shown the lines fill a square of 7.5cm (3in).
3 Carefully poke a hole at each of the points where the lines cross one another.
4 Fill this area with any kind of pattern, preferably starting at the centre and working outwards.

The example shown can be achieved by following steps 5–15.

Enlargement to show stitch positions (Steps 5–14, page 65).

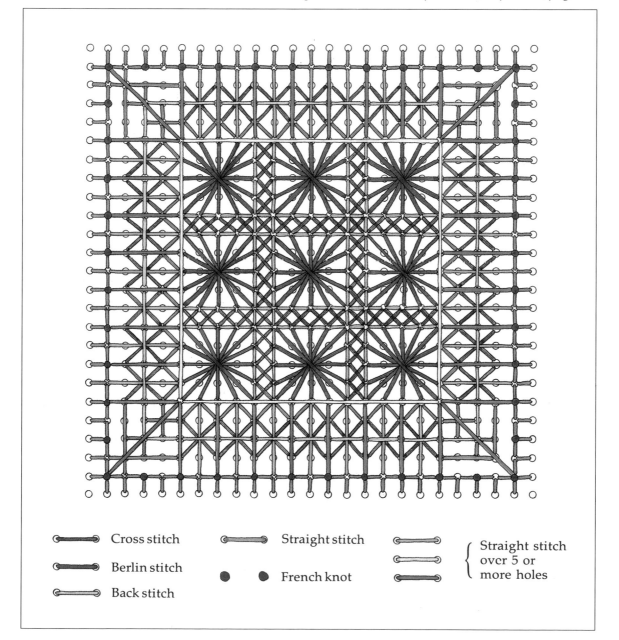

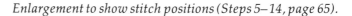 Cross stitch	Straight stitch
Berlin stitch	● ● French knot
Back stitch	{ Straight stitch over 5 or more holes

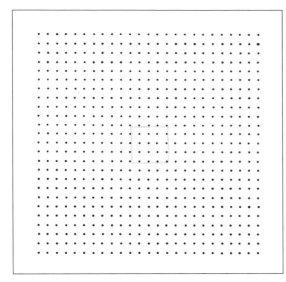

Step 5.

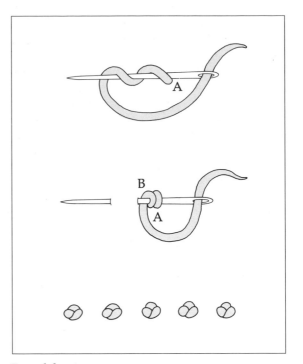

French knot.

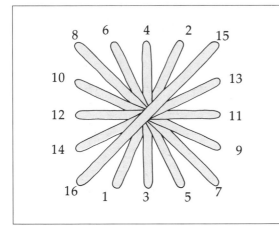

Berlin stitch.

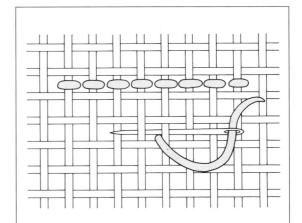

Back stitch.

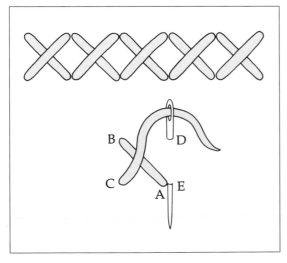

Cross stitch.

5 Locate the centre square consisting of 25 holes. Work one Berlin star stitch in yellow retors à broder.

6 Leave a gap around the first star and work eight further Berlin stars (to form a square covering 15 holes each way) in lime green retors à broder.

7 Two narrow strips of card space are now visible, in both directions, between the Berlin star squares. Fill these narrow gaps with cross stitch, in lemon perlé.

8 Still working on the same strips, work a row of back stitch down each side of the cross stitches, in green perlé.

9 Using back stitch once again, make a zig-zag lattice pattern, in dark green perlé, around the eight Berlin stars.

10 Continue the lattice, still in the same dark green, but use straight stitch to form the pattern, right up to the final edge.

11 Now, taking the lighter green perlé again, back stitch over the centres of the green crosses (using 3 holes).

12 Using a single strand of scarlet stranded cotton, make eight straight lines over 5 holes on each side of the Berlin star square. Add one diagonal stitch in each corner.

13 Using 3 strands of scarlet stranded cotton, put a French knot at the outside end of each of the scarlet lines.

14 Finally, finish with a single thread of lemon perlé over 15 holes on each side of the Berlin star square.

15 Lightly score the card for the fold. Bend in half. The back of the embroidery can be lined with a piece of fairly thick paper if a tidy finish is required.

Once you have the confidence, there is no end to the motifs that could be worked. These two additional motifs show simple patterns for a Christmas or Valentine card.

EMBROIDERED GREETINGS CARD (REPRESENTATIONAL)

Colour for this greeting card depends on the representation of a subject for its final outcome. Any subject will do – in this case it was a corner of a patch of rock roses. The starting point was a simple miniature painting but a photograph, preferably one's own, would be equally suitable.

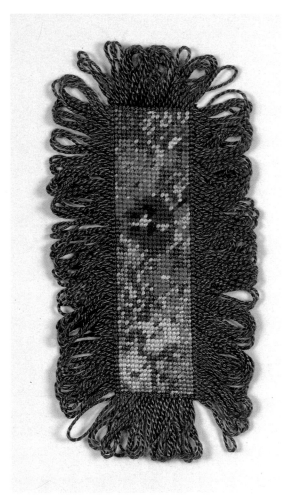

Materials

A suitable subject in the form of a painting or photograph

Tracing paper (of good quality, otherwise it is hard to see the painting underneath)

Canvas: single thread, 18 holes to 2.5cm (1in). A piece about 20 × 10cm (8 × 4in), or to fit available frame

Tapestry needle: size 20 or large enough to carry the thread with ease, but not so large that it distorts the canvas threads

Threads: DMC perlé cotton number 5. Colours used here are green 501, 580, 734; pinks 316, 814, 3350, 754, 899; yellow 445; orange 742; tan 402

Small rectangular embroidery frame over which to stretch the work whilst sewing

Masking tape

Drawing pins or staples if a conventional embroidery frame is not available

Fine black waterproof felt pen, and a fine ink pen

Odd strips of paper

One strip of card 2cm (¾in) wide

One piece of card out of which to make the greetings card itself, about 20 × 25cm (8 × 10in)

Glue, sticky tape and a small piece of lining paper for the back of the work are all optional

Method

1 Select an area of the painting or photograph about 9.5 × 2.5cm (3¾ × 1in) by means of masking with odd strips of paper, i.e. cover the areas not immediately required.

2 Mark the edges of this selected rectangle with ink.

3 Trace the main shape outlines with a fine ink line.

4 Lay the tracing on a clean, light-coloured surface.

5 Place a piece of canvas on top of the tracing. The black lines beneath should

An area of a small painting or photograph can be selected in order to produce an embroidery.

Steps 3–4.

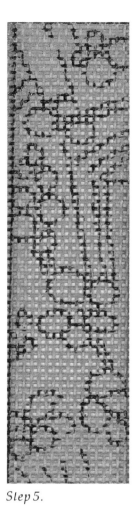

Step 5.

Tent stitch.

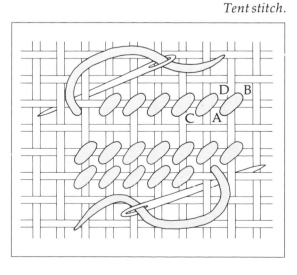

be clearly visible. Transpose these to the canvas with a waterproof black pen.

6 Fold masking tape over the raw edges of the canvas to prevent fraying.

7 Attach the canvas to a frame, (see pages 172–3).

8 Commence tent stitch, row by row, horizontally. Complete each row before moving to the next. Follow the painting as if by rows, keeping each coloured thread on the top surface of the work until required. This will save endless starting and finishing of colours and make it easy to re-introduce a colour, even for a single stitch, whenever required.

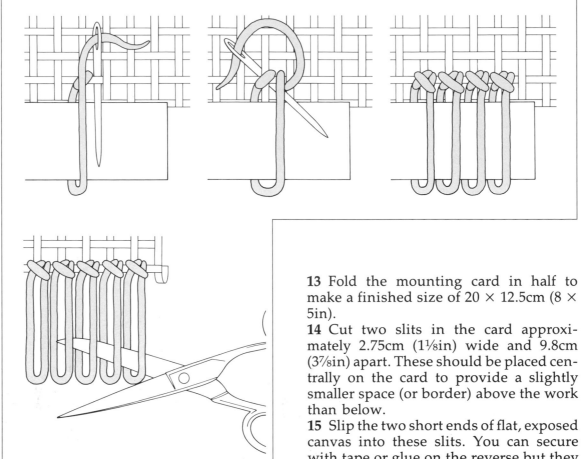

Velvet stitch.

13 Fold the mounting card in half to make a finished size of 20 × 12.5cm (8 × 5in).
14 Cut two slits in the card approximately 2.75cm (1⅛in) wide and 9.8cm (3⅞in) apart. These should be placed centrally on the card to provide a slightly smaller space (or border) above the work than below.
15 Slip the two short ends of flat, exposed canvas into these slits. You can secure with tape or glue on the reverse but they will hold quite well without.
16 The inside face of the card should be lined with a plain piece of paper.

Step 14.

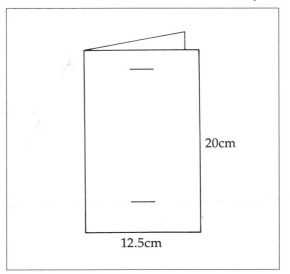

20cm

12.5cm

9 When the tent stitch is complete, prepare to make the velvet stitch fringe, by removing the work from the frame.
10 Trim the canvas so that 10 holes remain on the long edges and 20 holes on the two short edges.
11 Fold the lengthwise edge to the back of the work. Allow one un-embroidered thread and one hole of the canvas to remain on the front.
12 Commence the velvet stitch fringe, as shown in the diagram, along one of these lengthwise edges. Then continue around the short end in the same way but without bending the canvas to the back, i.e. keep the canvas of the two short ends out flat. Complete the velvet stitch border. The loops may be left as they are or cut, whichever you prefer.

Another idea for a similar use of a small-scale tent stitch embroidery is to substitute the final display card for a thick photographic print. Treat the photograph as a card window, mount and attach the embroidery (which should be a little larger than the hole in the mount) to the back (see page 179).

This chair seat lends itself particularly well to regular, geometric, abstract and symmetric treatment.

CHAIR SEAT

Embroidery on canvas can be pictorial, descriptive, organic and asymmetric. The chair seat, together with the tent stitch greetings card, illustrate, in their different ways, the hard-wearing practical potential of embroidery on canvas. Here, as in the card design, a ribbon effect is exploited. In direct contrast to the card design a single repeating geometric motif is used to build up the simplest pattern. This design was chosen because it reiterated the strip effect created by the slatted back of the chair.

The colours for such a design could be chosen from colours already in the room where the chair will be used. But it is sometimes a good idea to add one further colour that is not in the room to bring some additional life into the scheme. Keeping a notebook of such colour observations can be very useful.

Materials

Canvas: single thread, 12 holes to 2.5cm (1in), about 40 × 30cm (16 × 12in)

Masking tape to bind the raw edges of the canvas to prevent it from fraying

Rectangular embroidery frame, preferably large enough to carry the total number of embroidered strips

Drawing pins or staples, if a conventional frame is not available

Tapestry needle: size 16 (large enough to carry the threads but not so large that it will distort the canvas when going through)

Threads. DMC perlé cotton number 3: pink 963, one 45 metre ball used single will be enough for five strips 35.5cm (14in) in length. Perlé cotton number 5: buff 642, one 45 metre ball used as a double thread for each strip. Laine tapisserie: grey 7285, buff 7270, deep pink 7228, four to five 8 metre skeins per strip. Retors à broder number 4: orange 2740, one skein

Strip of card 2 × 38cm (¾ × 15in)

Furnishing fabric to cover the areas of the seat not embroidered

Upholstery tools and materials as required for the refurbishment and preparation of the chair itself

Method

1 Taking an area of canvas large enough for all the embroidered strips, mask the raw edges and mount onto the frame (see pages 172–3).

2 Mark out the position of each strip allowing about 5cm (2in) between each for cutting and seaming later.

3 Start in the centre of the canvas on the first unit.

4 Make one eastern stitch in pink perlé over two vertical and two horizontal threads of canvas.

Eastern stitch.

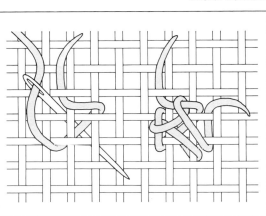

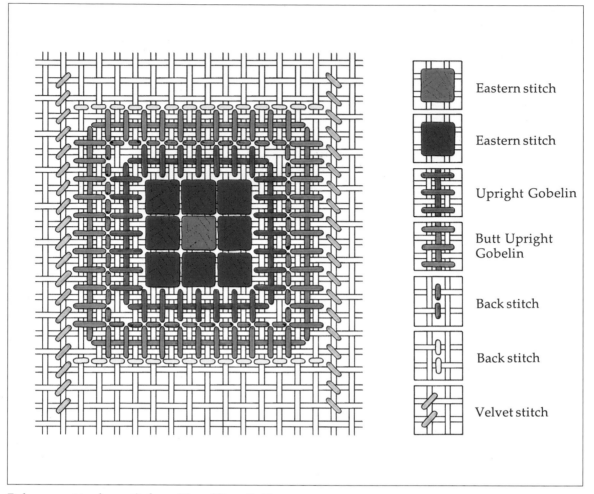

Eastern stitch

Eastern stitch

Upright Gobelin

Butt Upright Gobelin

Back stitch

Back stitch

Velvet stitch

Enlargement to show stitch positions (Steps 3–9).

5 Make a row of eight eastern stitches in grey wool around the central pink one. The embroidery will now be over a square block of six threads along each side of the square.

6 Using the deep pink wool, lay a straight line of wool over the eight threads on each of the four sides of the block. This thread will lie in the space between two parallel threads of canvas.

7 Now work gobelin stitch over this laid line in the same deep pink. The gobelin stitch will be over two threads of canvas and there will be seven stitches per side of the square block.

8 Repeat this same padded gobelin stitch in buff wool around the pink square; each

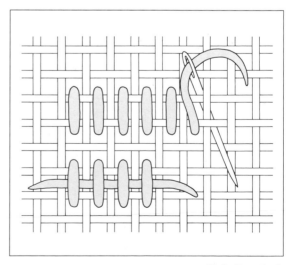

Gobelin stitch.

side of this new square will need eleven gobelin stitches.

9 Return to the pink perlé and back stitch between the two rows of gobelin stitch. To fully cover the corners a double stitch may be necessary.

10 Repeat this unit as many times as necessary. The chair illustrated has twelve units per strip.

11 When all units are complete in any one strip, use the orange retors à broder to separate the two rows of buff gobelin stitch using back stitch.

12 Fill in with two additional back stitches at the corners.

13 Work the velvet stitch fringe with a double thread of buff perlé cotton (see page 68).

14 Attach embroidery to fabric for seat cover and make up as required.

Detail of embroidery. It is always immensely satisfying to build a tiny unit of pattern with two or three, or at the most five, colours; especially if they are of varying thicknesses and types of thread.

CUSHION

Photography can play a large part in supplying and recording source material for designers. Further worlds open up to us when we look at the results of using a microscope in photography. Enlargements produce greater awareness of shapes, colours, lines and textures.

This cushion was inspired by a masterpiece of microscope photography: the camera image strongly suggested a textile interpretation.

Papilio Ulysses Linnaeus *by Kjell Sandved.*
Microscope photography at its finest in this
example of one of Kjell Sandved's studies of
butterflies.

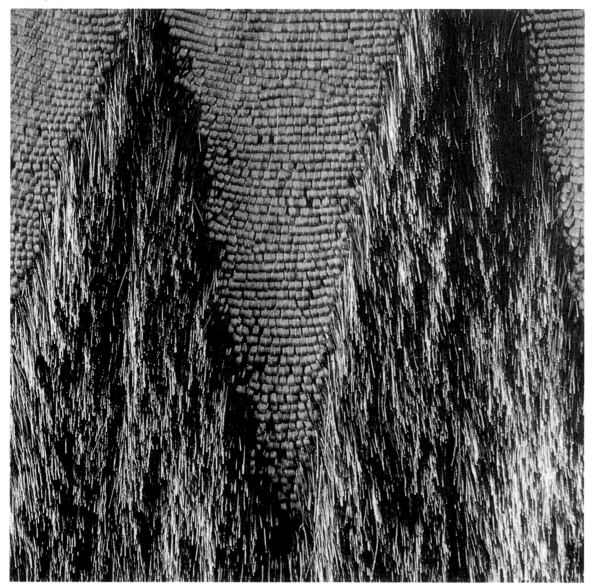

Materials

Canvas: 12 threads to 2.5cm (1in), about 45cm (18in) square

Threads. DMC stranded cotton: turquoise 995, 4 skeins. Buffs 612, 3023, pink 3687, 12 skeins of each. Laine tapisserie: 7488, two 8 metre skeins for back stitching. 7319 for tramming under the gobelin (certain double knitting wools would do well as a substitute), one skein. Coton à broder: 319 dark green

Tapestry needle

Masking tape for binding the raw edges of the canvas to prevent fraying

Rectangular frame large enough to carry the whole area of canvas to be embroidered

Drawing pins or staples, to attach the canvas to the frame if a conventional frame is not being used

Fabric such as velvet or leather to complete the cushion

Sewing cotton to match the fabric

Strip of card 33 × 2cm (13 × ¾in)

Black waterproof pen

Oddment of paper

Method

1 Start with a 30.5cm (12in) square of paper. Cut into it from one edge by making a series of different sized triangles. Do this with reference to the paper exercises on page 5. In this example the paper has simply been divided in two. Several attempts at cutting may be necessary to get a visually comfortable result that has a good balance between both sections of the paper.

2 Take the square of canvas and bind all the raw edges.

3 Lay it on a flat surface and place the interlocking parts of the paper square centrally on it.

4 With a waterproof pen mark the position of the 30.5cm (12in) square and the zig-zag line of the paper pattern that divides the area.

5 Attach the canvas to the frame (see pages 172–3).

6 Work first one half then the other half of the embroidery.

7 Proceed row by row to cover one half in upright gobelin stitch (see page 72). Use dark blue laine tapisserie as the laid thread, overlaid with all six strands of turquoise stranded cotton.

8 Between each row of gobelin stitch work a row of back stitch (see page 64) in brown laine tapisserie.

9 Cover the remaining portion of the work with multi-coloured velvet stitch (see page 68) using the strip of card to regulate the length of the pile.

In order to achieve the multi-coloured effect shown, the needle has been threaded with two strands of each of the two buff and one pink stranded cottons together with one thickness of green coton à broder. Great variety is attainable by the regrouping of threads.

When working an area of velvet stitch, rather than producing it as a single line, it is essential to work the stitch from the bottom of the work upwards. (In this case from the narrow points to the widest parts.) This keeps the long threads out of the way of the next line of stitches. The

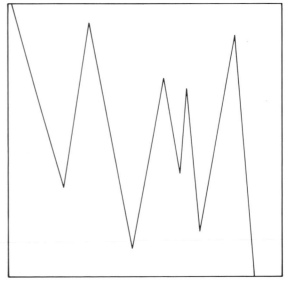

Step 1.

loops in this case have been cut. Variety can be achieved by simply varying the loop lengths or by mixing cut and uncut loops.

10 Remove the work from the frame and stretch (see page 176).

11 Make up the cushion as required. Try using a contrasting material such as velvet (as here) or leather; but any strong, firm fabric which will support the heavily embroidered canvas would be fine.

Detail of finished embroidery.

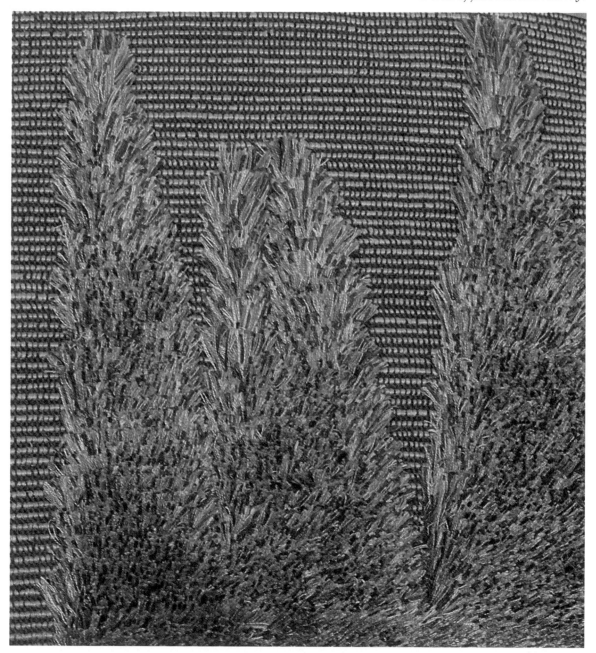

SECTION 4: TEXTURE

The definition of texture lies in the intrinsic quality of a surface. It may be spongy, furry, sticky, slimy, smooth, spiky, lumpy, silky, gritty, etc. It can be experienced with the eyes shut; it is tactile and therefore a concept of touch. The ability to recognise and appreciate texture comes naturally to children but is a skill that may have to be re-learnt as an adult.

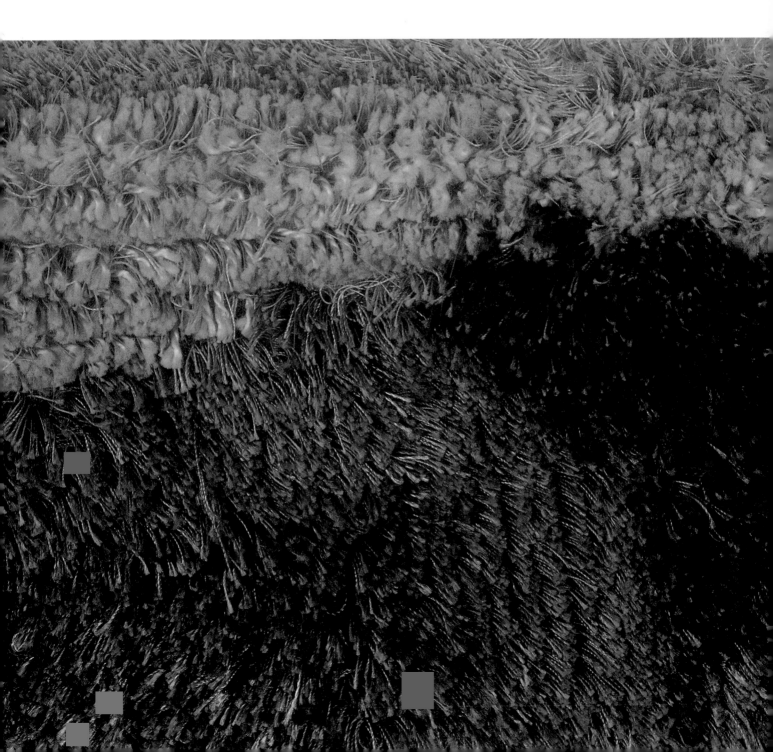

Thread of almost any sort is an ideal medium for the creation of texture. Contrasts of thread type combined with different methods of application can produce an unending variety of results. The creation of texture using embroidery thread is particularly pleasurable as it can be additionally enjoyed for its visual, non-compositional (that is, without a focal point), all-over surface.

Painting and photography cannot produce an actual texture of an observed subject, but they can imply the qualities of surface.

LEFT: *This sample was made with a variety of cotton and rayon machine embroidery threads using an industrial tufting machine. The use of colour adds to the overall effect.*

ABOVE: *Photograph showing the textural quality of a cat's fur. It can be very helpful to keep both a visual and actual scrapbook of textures that have particular appeal for you.*

A SMALL TEXTURED PICTURE

A simple exercise that can be very rewarding is to get a photograph that implies a texture of some kind and then decide in what way the photographic subject could be made tactile.

This approach to decision making is ideal for those who do not wish to draw or paint as it is instantaneous and exciting. It also avoids any apprehension that newcomers to drawing and painting may feel. The design problem is limited to simply what stitch, what colour, what type of thread and on what scale.

LEFT: *Paintings, too, can be added to the scrapbook. Notice how this one captures something of the crisp, dry and brittle quality of the protea's petals and leaves.*

BELOW: Landscape *by John Hunnex. This photograph was selected because of its dominant textural foreground which provided the stimulus and visual support for further enrichment.*

Materials

A good photograph; preferably on good photographic paper which is strong enough to support the stitchery. However if the paper is thin, then the image should first be pasted onto good quality drawing paper. Allow the glue to dry before attempting to sew!

Threads. DMC perlé cotton in all three weights 3, 5 and 8 (thick, medium and fine). Colours: fawns 640, 642, 644; salmons 948, 353; pale pink 819; dark brown 3371

Crewel needles (assorted packet)

Sharp scissors

Method

1 Select one stitch and practise it on a spare piece of fabric or paper. Choose one that best expresses the surface portrayed.

For the beginner it is usually better to use only one stitch on one piece of work and apply it satisfactorily rather than attempt many stitches and create a visual muddle. The choice of stitch in this case was clipped herringbone.

2 Carefully consider which areas of the picture will be worked. Then consider where to use similar colours to the photograph and which areas might benefit from the addition of a new colour.

3 If the stitch selected is normally worked in a line then decide the direction of these lines on the picture.

4 Try and decide whether the stitch selected could, in certain treatments, lose its linear dominance and be worked to give an overall texture.

5 When the picture is complete, mount it (see page 179).

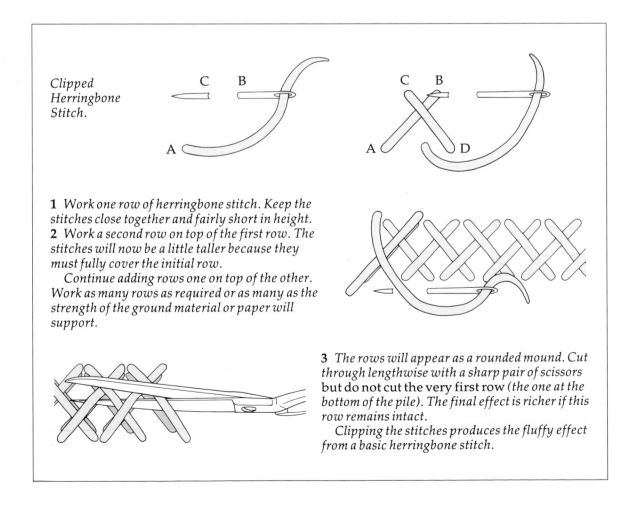

Clipped Herringbone Stitch.

1 *Work one row of herringbone stitch. Keep the stitches close together and fairly short in height.*
2 *Work a second row on top of the first row. The stitches will now be a little taller because they must fully cover the initial row.*

Continue adding rows one on top of the other. Work as many rows as required or as many as the strength of the ground material or paper will support.

3 *The rows will appear as a rounded mound. Cut through lengthwise with a sharp pair of scissors but do not cut the very first row (the one at the bottom of the pile). The final effect is richer if this row remains intact.*

Clipping the stitches produces the fluffy effect from a basic herringbone stitch.

Photograph with embroidery superimposed.
In spite of the provision of a complete image,
much inventiveness is still demanded from the
embroiderer.

MAKING A TEXTURED SURFACE WITH A LOOP PILE NEEDLE

This exercise illustrates the simple pleasure to be gained by creating a richly textured surface using different threads: in particular, the combining and contrasting of varying types of yarn using a loop pile needle. This tool can produce striking and fascinating textures. The addition of colour, combined with four possible lengths of loop (cut later if desired) can provide an utterly absorbing occupation.

A loop pile needle threaded with varying mixtures of odd knitting wools, tapestry wool and perlé cotton, produces this tufted effect.

Materials

Rectangular frame

Staples or strips of carpet tacking (strips of wood with numerous very sharp imbedded spikes)

Evenweave fabric or hessian: any type a littler larger than the frame

Loop pile needle (see Suppliers' List, page 182).

Tapestry needle for threading the loop pile needle. The eye must be large enough to carry the desired threads but not so large that it will not pass through the eye of the looper

White latex adhesive. (Spray glues are also successful. See Suppliers' List, page 182).

Threads. Almost anything is suitable. The work illustrated includes some of the following.

Oddments of knitting yarn (wool and synthetic, both 3 and 4 ply). The tool is greedy with thread so remainders are useful. DMC perlé cotton number 8 in black. These samples together with the cat bag on pages 87–9 have absorbed about 300gms. Perlé cotton number 5: 977 and 920, three 25m skeins of each. Laine tapisserie: 7169 and 7176, six 25m skeins of each. This yarn is made up of four strands which have been carefully parted for this project. These single threads have then been wound onto a cotton reel. The knots formed by joining the lengths together do not matter as they will slip easily through the eye of the looper. Stranded cotton: several skeins have been used in each of the following colours, rainbow colours 69, 51, 105; others 951, 402, 918, 356, 922

Weaving gimp

Weaving cotton (matt)

Sharp scissors

Method

1 Stretch the fabric over the frame. Attach with staples or carpet strip (see pages 172–3). The material should be as taut as possible in order to achieve a regular loop.

2 The loop pile needle has four small holes for the selection of the loop length. To change from one to the other the screw has to be removed and replaced in the appropriate position.

3 To thread the needle, always bring the winding handle and the protruding set of four holes to a position nearest the main handle. This retracts the inner tongue of the hollow needle.

4 Thread the sewing needle with the chosen yarn or group of yarns. Hold the looper in one hand and with the other hand pass the threaded sewing needle in a downward direction through the eye of the looper.

5 Whilst keeping the looper in the position as described in 3 above, place it at right angles to the reverse side of the fabric.

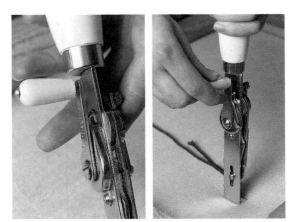

Step 3.   Steps 5–6.

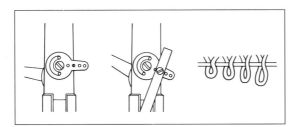

Loop pile needle (Step 2).

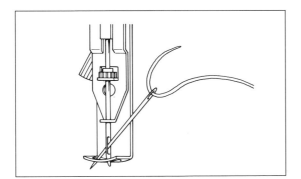

Threading the loop pile needle (Step 4).

6 Before starting to wind the handle, make sure that the short spare end of the thread is well clear of the looper otherwise it will quickly be re-absorbed by the looper and create a tangle.

7 All threads to be fed into the needle at any one time should be contained in separate bowls or boxes on the floor immediately beneath the frame. This is essential in order to maintain a clear uninterrupted flow of yarn to the looper. It also prevents the different yarns from becoming tangled.

8 When a row of tufting is complete, cut the ends of the yarn close to the fabric. If this is not done they have a habit of straying back and becoming entangled with the looper. If stray ends do get caught the work will unravel.

9 Easy unravelling can be an advantage because if a mistake is made the yarn can be pulled out and reused.

10 Continue to make rows in any order, direction or length.

11 When the area is complete, place a thin layer of latex adhesive all over the back of the work. This will permanently secure the threads in place. Allow to dry.

12 Remove from the frame. Clip or trim loops if desired.

13 The fabric is now ready to use.

CAT BAG

There are many different textural effects or 'fabrics' that can be made by experimenting with the looper.

To make a finished article you will need to make enough loop-pile fabrics or surfaces to form any relevant shapes.

Colour is also important in achieving a textural effect with the looper. In this example the colours were selected to suggest a tortoiseshell or marmalade cat.

This idea can be developed further to make the kind of zipped bag that children love to keep their treasures in.

With little effort and lots of yarn, a tufted fabric can be created to suit any item, from a carpet to a toy cat.

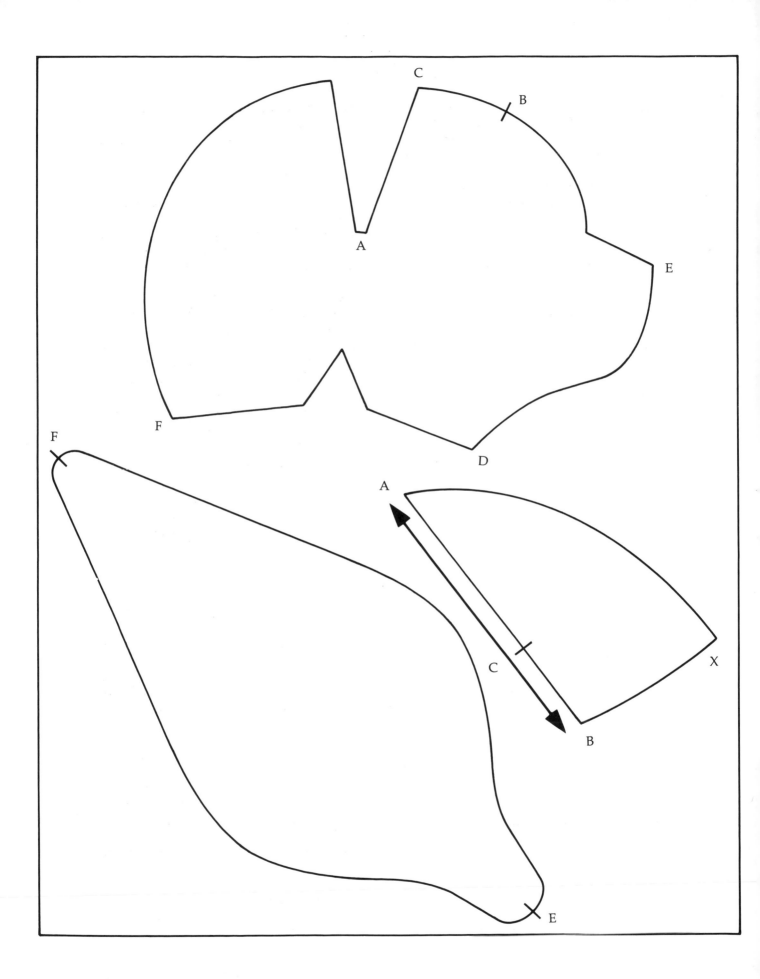

Materials

A selection of loop pile textured fabrics

Pattern for the toy or other article. A simple cat head pattern is included here but the feet, tail and flat body are all shapes that have been left to the individual's imagination

Felt, in a matching colour (used for the underside of the bag, the tail and feet)

Lining material (ordinary curtain lining has been used to provide a soft inner lining to the bag). (The reverse side of loop pile work tends to be rather rough if left unbacked)

Zip (a little smaller than the width of the bag. It should be inserted about 10cm (4in) in from the head end of the felt underside of the bag)

Eyes and whiskers obtainable from shops selling toy-making accessories

Strong sewing cotton

Sewing needles

Pins

Scissors

Wadding for the head

Method

To make the head:

1 Lay the pattern pieces on the reverse side of the textured fabric.

2 Add about 2mm ($\frac{1}{8}$in) for the seam and cut out.

3 Remember to turn the pattern over when cutting the second side of the head and the second ear. (Cut two pieces for the ear before turning the pattern over to cut two more pieces.)

4 Place two pieces of one ear right sides together. With small overcasting stitches, sew A to X and X to B. The unstitched inside edge AB allows for turning to the right side again. Repeat for second ear.

5 Place each ear in turn into the V-shaped dart in each side of the head, matching points A to C. Fold the head piece in half to sandwich the ear. (All four edges should be at the same level and can be easily overcast.) Stitch.

6 Once again, fold each head section to allow the small V-shaped neck dart to come right sides together. Overcast with small stitches.

7 Place the two sides of the head with right sides facing, and stitch between points D and E.

8 Tack the protruding unsewn edge of the ear CB to the points CB on the head section.

9 With right sides together, sew each side of head gusset to each top edge of head sections between points E to B and C to F.

10 Attach whiskers and eyes.

11 Stuff carefully with wadding and sew up remaining seam as invisibly as possible. This seam should allow two points to protrude which can easily be attached to the surface of the bag. A third point of attachment will be needed at the lower back of the head using a few firm stitches.

12 Add any additional thick wool stitchery to mark the mouth and nose.

To make the rest of body and bag:

13 Four feet and a tail can be made with either two layers of the loop pile texture, as with the ears, or using a piece of felt instead of one of the textured pieces.

14 A simple bag can be made in the same way but you will need a larger seam allowance than allowed on the head pieces. The textured area to be used for the bag should first be lined with a soft, strong lining fabric.

15 Next, the four feet and tail should be tacked into position on the seam line of the upper textured fabric. The feet and tail will require adequate seam allowances to match those of the bag. Place with their right sides facing the right side of the bag, and stitch.

16 The felt under-fabric of the bag should be cut large enough to allow for the zip to be inserted in the conventional way.

17 With the zip inserted, place right sides of both parts of the bag together. Stitch all round with a back stitch, by hand (the fabric will be too thick for most machines).

18 Using the zip opening, turn the work to the right side.

19 Finally, attach the head with a few strong stitches as in step 11.

Finer and more delicate effects of colour are
easily attainable with the same loop pile needle.
This example shows how the same tool, but here
filled with stranded cottons, silks and rayon
yarns, can produce such different results. The
work contains the contrasting use of the looper at
both its lowest and highest setting of loop length
and shows the decorative value of cut and uncut
loops.

The colours were chosen and the techniques
developed to capture the essence of the raked
lines of gravel around the pompom bushes of a
Japanese Zen garden in autumn. It is one in a
series of twelve decorative panels based on the
theme of the Japanese garden in all seasons.

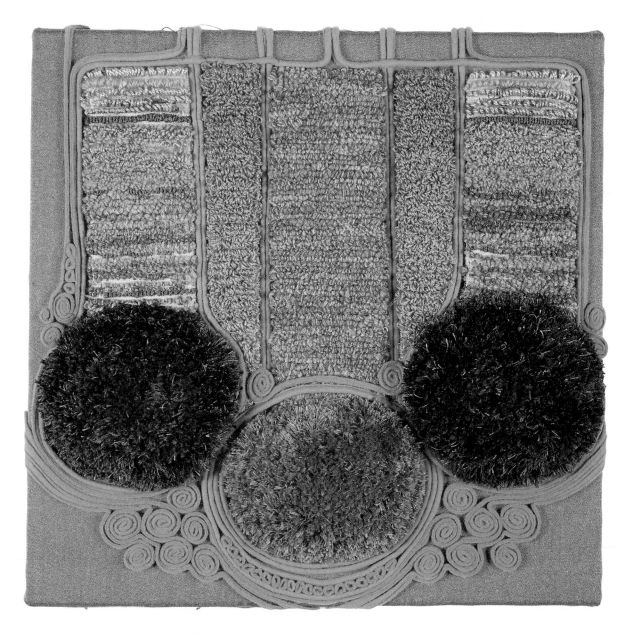

*This simple painting of fallen cherry leaves and
thyme bushes in autumn provided the inspiration
for the three embroidered interpretations that
follow.*

Texture in thread does not always have to be raised, looped or shaggy. It can find equally rich expression in fine low-lying treatments. These three samples show machine embroidery cotton used in a fairly uniform manner on an industrial Cornelly machine (chain stitch machine).

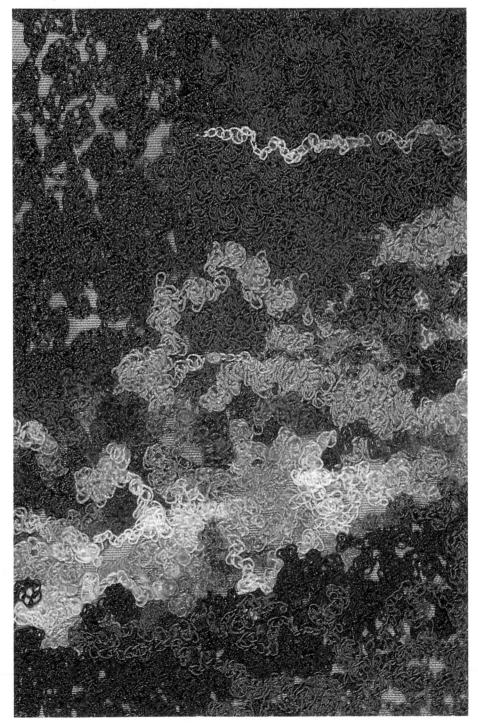

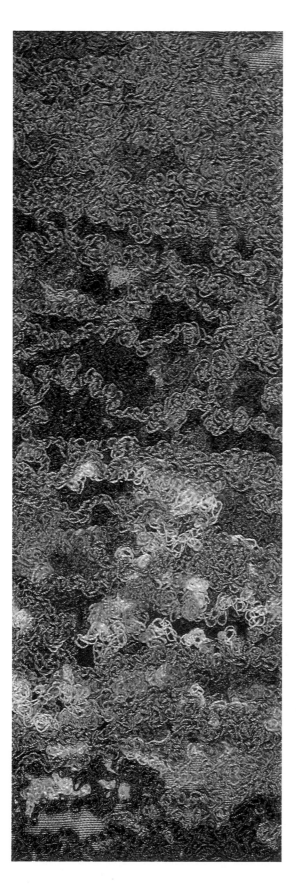

SECTION 5: PATTERN

Pattern is most easily recognised when shapes or lines, or a combination of the two, are repeated; but pattern can also be non-repeating.

Pattern of some kind occurs in most man-made and natural objects and our environment is very rich in both types. Man-made examples include patterned carpets, wrought iron, ceramics, wood carving and illuminated manuscripts. Such patterns found in applied art can in turn be compared with works of fine art: the paintings of Matisse, both abstract and representational, are total expressions of pattern.

Compare these two contrasting styles of man-made pattern: the geometric, abstract decoration of an English Art Deco decanter and the organic, representational ornamentation of a late eighteenth century Wedgwood teapot.

LEFT: *Papua New Guinea man. Adorning the human body can also produce rich pattern combinations of shape, colour and line.*

BELOW: *Making paintings of everyday objects around the house helps to build up a useful notebook of patterns.*

The natural world is prolific as a source of pattern, for example the coat of a tortoiseshell cat, the skin of a snake, the feathers of a guinea fowl and the variegated leaves of plants.

CLOTHES COVER

Many people collect an assortment of fabric scraps and bits and pieces of lace. Lace can add greatly to a mixed fabric project as in this example which combines lace with a royal blue silk; the two uniting to produce a simple repeating pattern.

The pattern has been achieved using 149 small units of traditional English Suffolk Puff patchwork – also known as Yorkshire Daisy, Puff Ball or Yo-Yo. These small circles have been used side by side and overlapped, sometimes lined with lace, edged with lace or folded in half – the variations are limitless.

Silk and lace clothes cover. By using a different colour of silk it could become a cot coverlet. By gracious permission of HRH Princess Alice Duchess of Gloucester.

Materials

Oddments of lace

0.5m (⅗yd) fabric: something delicate like silk, cotton, organdie or voile is best for this technique as it will provide a good support in terms of texture and weight when combined with lace

Matching sewing cotton

Sewing needles

Sharp scissors

Fabric for lining the back of the work. Here a cream satin was used as the work was made up as a lingerie cover. The design could also be made into a bag for stockings, night-clothes, etc., when matching fabric may be suitable

Rectangular embroidery frame (optional)

Method

To make a Suffolk Puff:

1 Cut a circle of fabric twice as large as the required puff, in this case diameter 3.75cm (1½in).

2 Begin by turning the edge of the circle to the inside. Fold only a very small amount.

3 Sew using running stitch. Only attempt to hold a tiny amount of turned fabric with the thumb and then catch the next little prepared piece with a stitch.

4 Gather this row of running stitch fairly tightly and evenly. Secure the thread invisibly with a few overcast stitches.

5 When a number of puffs are complete, experiment with the arrangement of these units to form simple repeating patterns: in this case on a ground fabric.

6 Before applying the puffs to their final position on the ground fabric it is often easier to mount this base material onto a frame of some kind (see pages 172–3).

7 Traditionally, Suffolk Puffs are sewn edge to edge using small overcasting stitches.

8 Make up into a cover, a bag, or as required.

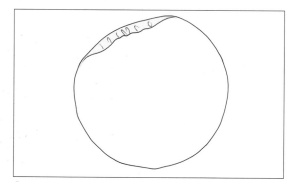

Steps 1–2.

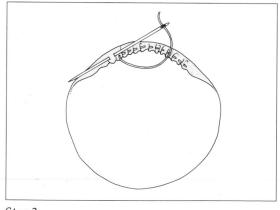

Step 3.

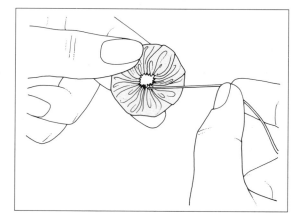

Step 4.

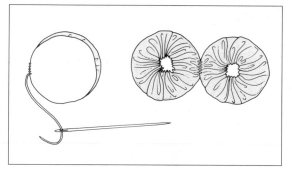

Step 7.

*Patchwork cushion. This design is based on an
adaptation of the 'Log Cabin' technique which is
thought to have originated in Canada.*

PATCHWORK CUSHION

Sometimes an embroiderer will be commissioned to design a work that must include a range of disparate colours (as happened recently to me with a commission from the University of Sheffield that required me to include the fourteen colours of the academic hoods).

Anyone who has taken part in a group project will have experienced this design problem. It is not always easy to resolve, but often the challenge can in itself prove stimulating and rewarding.

This is a small-scale project, but the method of approach could well be applied to something much larger. Note that the different colours have been separated by alternate piped strips of grey.

Materials

30cm (12in) square of soft plain backing material; fine bleached calico is suitable

Pencil and ruler

Sharp scissors

Needles and pins

Coloured fabric pieces; the ones used here are all in fine silk

Matching sewing cottons

About 20m (22yd) piping cord, size 00. If the actual edge of the cushion is to be piped more cord will be required

Sewing machine with a zipper foot

Method

1 With a pencil, draw two diagonals across the square of backing fabric.

2 Draw a 5cm (2in) square in the centre.

3 Add a further three squares around this central square increasing each by 2.5cm (1in).

4 Cut a 5cm (2in) square of coloured fabric and tack it in the central position.

5 The next step is to make the piped fabric strips so that they are ready to apply onto the ground fabric. Consider in which order to place the different colours. Fabrics should be cut into 3cm (1¼in)

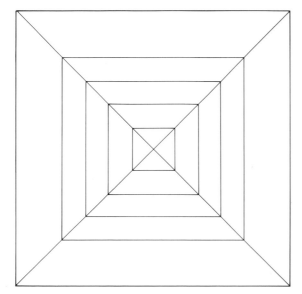

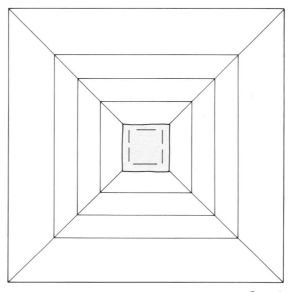

Steps 1–3.   *Step 4.*

width strips. The lengths should correspond to the lengths of the sides of each
square, i.e. 10cm (4in), 15cm (6in), 20.3cm
(8in), PLUS a 1cm (½in) turnings allowance *at each end.*

6 Starting with the colours that will form
the sides of the smallest inner square,
plan and make a group of nine piped
strips.

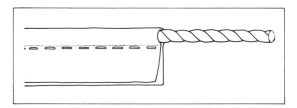

Steps 7–8.

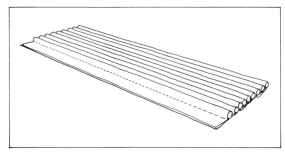

Step 9.

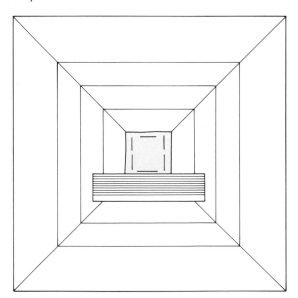

Step 11.

7 Fold the fabric strip in half lengthwise
around the piping cord.

8 Using a zipper foot, machine with a
very short stitch-length right up against
the cord.

9 Stitch these nine piped cords side by
side; one at a time, with the raw edges
overlapping.

10 Remove piping cord from each strip
and press. It is advisable not to remove
the cord *before* stitching the group
together because the cord acts as a good
guide for a straight machine line. These
nine lengths of piping cord could be
reused, in turn, on the other three sides. If
you use new cords for every strip, collect
them at the end of the project ready to
make the next cushion!

The planning and composition of the
work can be made much easier if all the
strips for one side are made before going
on to make the strips for another side.

11 When all four groups of strips belong-
ing to the 10cm (4in) square are complete,
lay one of these strips in position on the
backing fabric. The piped edge should
overlap the centre square by 5mm (¼in)
and overhang the sides of the centre
square by 1cm (½in) on each side.

12 By hand, stitch the leading edge invisibly to the ground fabric.

13 Stitch the raw edge by hand.

14 Proceed with the other three sides in
turn, in the same way.

15 Repeat the same sequence when applying the four medium and the four
large piped strips onto the corresponding
middle and outside squares.

16 Cut four pieces of fabric, 30.5 × 7.5cm
(12 × 3in), for the surrounding ground.
Silk was used here.

17 With right sides facing, place two
strips of fabric on opposite sides of the
piped square. Pin, tack and then machine
along the stitch line of the outermost line
of piping.

18 Open these two strips to their right
sides and press so that they lie flat with
the decorative patchwork.

19 Repeat for the other two fabric strips.

20 Make up the cushion as required.

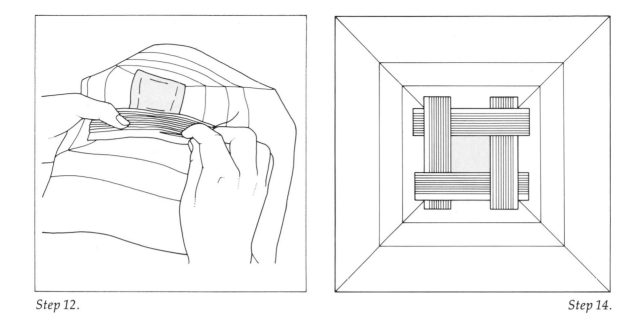

Step 12.

Step 14.

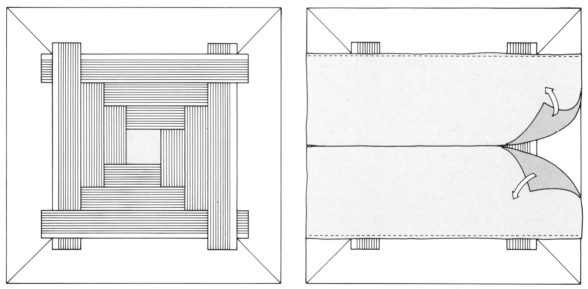

Step 15.

Step 17.

*Adding four strips of grey silk, to complete the
cushion cover.*

There are many different arrangements of pattern that can evolve from the same set of colours. Simply by altering the role of the grey stripe, the pattern can completely change in character: here the grey is used as just another colour. The rotation of the central band of piping to form a diamond shape is a further development of the pattern.

WAISTCOAT

The camera is a very satisfactory way of recording visual material. Photographs of the painted patterns on Chinese architecture provided the starting point for the patchwork waistcoat shown on page 110. It is important to stress that only the essence of the coloured shapes and forms have been extracted; the photographs have not been slavishly copied but used instead as a reminder of the oscillations and juxtapositions of an almost jewelled heaven. The subject offers a rich example of coloured shape and form. It is a good idea to make many simple sponge paintings before deciding on the final sheet of patterns.

Richly patterned and painted ceilings in Beijing, China.

Patchwork waistcoat based on painted ceiling patterns; very similar to the intricate patterns created by a child's kaleidoscope.

Materials

Lots of sheets of paper of any quality

Water-based paints – tubes are much easier to handle than pots or hard blocks. Gouache is lovely to use, but expensive

Pot of water

2.5cm (1in) cube of sponge

A selection of fabric pieces on which to base the painted design and from which the patchwork will be made. The colours could relate directly to those of the observed subject or could be a selection of them

Tracing paper

Pencil and ruler

Black ball-point or felt-tipped pen

Heavy sew-in Vilene: about 60cm (2ft) square

Lining for the waistcoat

Pattern for the waistcoat. The pattern provided around the painting is to scale and could be enlarged as required

Additional fabric in one of the patchwork colours to make an edge binding

Waistcoat buckle

Matching sewing cottons

Fine sewing needles

Pins

The simple painted marks of the final choice of sponge painting.

Method

1 Select a group of fabrics that will form the basis of the colours to be used for the design.

2 With these in mind, start to freely paint patterns, using the sponge. Base these free movements on some observed pattern source and paint simply (see page 13).

3 Several attempts may be necessary in order to achieve a final and satisfactory result. In this case satisfactory means a

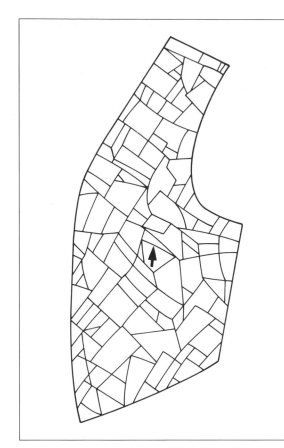

Step 5.

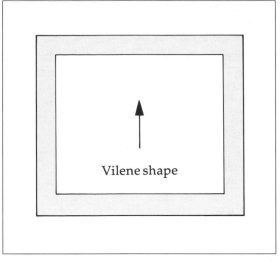

Step 10.

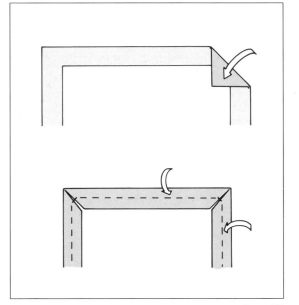

Step 15.

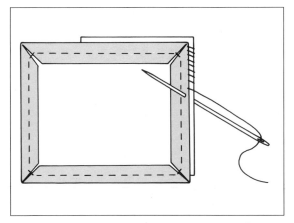

Step 16.

pattern that is of a scale and character that could be worn: a pattern that is not too complicated to transpose to patchwork; and a pattern where the choice and balance of colour have been carefully considered.

4 When the final painting is dry, take a ball-point pen and outline the different coloured shapes. It is important to clearly define the perimeter of each little coloured area.

5 Carefully trace the painting. It is important at this stage to eliminate any shapes that will be very awkward to cut out, for example, narrow points that will simply fall apart when cut in fabric.

6 Lay the tracing over a sheet of white paper which will throw the pencil lines into greater contrast. Over this lay a piece of Vilene.

7 Trace the lines once again using a ball-point pen.

8 Turn the tracing paper over and use it to make a second image, this time reversed, onto a second piece of Vilene.

9 Mark on each Vilene tracing the right and the left sides of the waistcoat.

10 On the Vilene tracing mark every little shape with a vertical arrow to denote the eventual straight grain of the fabric.

11 Using the painting as a colour chart, systematically use the Vilene shapes as templates for the construction of the patchwork. Work as follows:

12 Cut only one shape from the Vilene at a time.

13 Take this shape and lay it, arrow on underside, on the back of the fabric to be used for the patch. The arrow should run in the same direction as the straight grain of the fabric.

14 Cut out around the Vilene shape but leave 5mm (¼in) for the turnings.

15 Turn the edges of the fabric to the wrong side and invisibly catch stitch to the Vilene in such a way that the thread does not go through to the right side of the fabric. Corners are best folded as in the diagram.

16 As each shape is prepared, sew it to its neighbour, right sides facing, using small overcasting stitches.

17 Press gently.

18 When the patchwork for both fronts is complete, make up the garment following pattern instructions.

Detail of waistcoat.

SWEATER

The patchwork for the design for a sweater (shown on page 116) was inspired by the patterns found on Chinese screens.

In China, screens are placed in gardens and used to frame patches of colour and beautiful details of shape.

Sweater with patchwork bands.

The decorative bands of patchwork in this sweater provide ribbons of shapes which become flat insertions of colour trapped between the knitted seams of the sweater. Sewing the seams of any knitted garment can be tedious; the inclusion of a decorative band makes the finishing of the garment part of the creative process.

The initial unit of patchwork, in this case 63.5cm (25in), can be repeated often enough to equal the length and number of seams that will carry an inset. In this example, 48cm (19in) of patchwork was required for each side seam, 58.5cm (23in) for around each armhole and the underarm seams required a further 63.5cm (25in) each.

The strip of colour is only 5cm (2in) wide and the number of colours has been limited to four: brown, dark charcoal grey, silver grey and red.

When knitting the garment remember to deduct the width of the patchwork strip from the width of the knitting. For example, if a 112cm (44in) chest size is required then only cast on the number of stitches specified for the 102cm (40in) size.

Materials
For the knitting:
Any knitting pattern, but the sweater shown is Studio Number 22 from the *Rowan Knitting Book Number 1*.
Knitting needles; sizes 9 (3¾mm) and 7 (4½mm)
Stitch holders: 4 or 5
Wool. Sweater here knitted in Rowan Spun Tweed in black with a multi-coloured fleck. (Seven 100gm hanks were needed for a 112cm (44in) chest.)
For the patchwork:
Water-based paints
Paper
Waterpot
Sponge or brushes
Odd strips of paper
Pins
Good quality tracing paper
Firm iron-on Vilene; enough to provide complete lengths for each patchwork strip
Fabric pieces for the patchwork. Here Viyella, pure cotton and Dupion have

been used. If you choose a fabric which frays badly, back it with Soft iron-on Vilene before attempting to cut out any shapes
Matching sewing cottons
Soft pencil
Small sharp scissors
Sewing needles

Method
1 Select a suitable subject using photographs or a suitable painting.
2 Paint a simple pattern using the chosen fabrics as the basis for the colours; these can, of course, be different from the original subject source. Paint freely on a piece of paper considerably larger than the strip which will eventually be required. Make several paintings to allow for some choice.
3 Place four odd strips of paper on the painting to frame the shape and size of the pattern required.

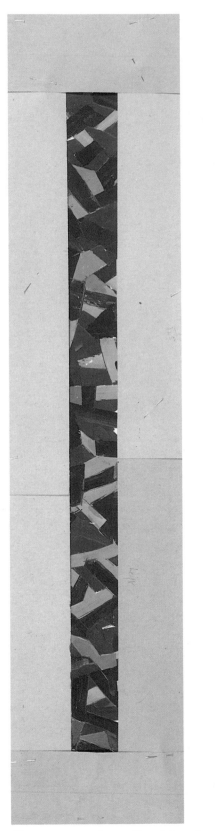

Chosen pattern framed by strips of paper, then traced (Steps 3–4).

4 Lay the tracing paper over the painting and trace with a pencil. Select the most obvious, most easily defined and most suitable shapes for patchwork.

This kind of tracing can be very creative; it need not be a copy of everything that can be seen underneath! In other words, there is no point in recording tiny, unworkable cracks of colour or narrow impossible shapes – interpret intelligently.

5 Prepare strips of Firm iron-on Vilene the length and width required for each strip of decoration.

6 Turn the tracing face downwards on a light-coloured ground; the lighter this surface is, the easier it is to achieve the next step.

7 Lay a Vilene strip, sticky side down, on top of the tracing, and transpose the lines to the Vilene with a soft pencil.

8 Repeat this last process to correspond with the number of patchwork strips required.

9 Mark each shape on the Vilene tracing with an arrow to indicate the vertical direction of the shape (see page 112).

10 Cut out one shape from the Vilene strip. Place this, glue side down, on the wrong side of the patch fabric, matching the arrow with the straight grain of the fabric.

11 Carefully iron on. (Do not make the iron too hot. Every iron is different, so it is prudent to try various heats on a spare piece of fabric.)

12 Cut out leaving a 5mm (¼in) allowance for the turnings.

13 Carefully turn the edges of the fabric to the wrong side and catch stitch invisibly to the Vilene.

14 As each shape is prepared, sew it to its neighbour, right sides facing, using small overcasting stitches.

15 When all the strips have been worked, press lightly before inserting into the knitting. Use small overcasting stitches to attach to the sweater seams.

16 The back of the patchwork has been lined with a piece of black cotton curtain lining. This is optional, but makes a perfect finish.

Detail of patchwork insert.

SECTION 6: FORM

Form is the word used to describe something three dimensional, for example, the human form.

Form is sculptural and in the round, so can be applied to almost everything we see from a building to a cabbage. Every subject offers infinite interpretation. Each of us will relate to, and prefer, quite different things. These will need to be recorded in some way, either by taking photos, making drawings or paintings or by collecting interesting pictures from magazines and newspapers.

Wherever we look, form is anywhere and everywhere; we simply have to select what appeals the most.

*Holiday photos can provide useful records of
suitable subjects, for example, the striking form
of a basket of lotus flowers or a seagull at feeding
time.*

Few forms could be larger or more magnificent than the rocks of the Stone Forest in south-west China (LEFT). Compare these pointed, angular sculptures with the majestic, rounded forms of the rocks off the coast of the Scilly Isles in the gouache painting made with sponge and brush below.

SOFT TOY OR CUSHION

This design was developed from numerous sketches of Rhode Island chickens. The simple form of the hen has been interpreted in many piped felt strips of different colours and lengths applied to a felt ground. The idea could be extended to all kinds of birds and animals and could be developed into a larger scale group project.

Materials

For one chicken 33cm (width) × 35.5cm (height) (13 × 14in):

Photograph or painting of a chosen subject

Tracing paper

Pencil

French chalk or talcum powder

Small pad of felt (or similar) with which to apply the chalk

Small paint brush (number 1 sable is best)

Water-based white paint

Needle (fairly large)

Felt: small areas of 10 different colours have been used in this example, plus two 38cm (15in) squares for the ground material and backing

Matching sewing cottons

Piping cord: number 3, about 12m (13yd). Number 2, about 1m (1yd) for the finer details of the head

Sharp scissors

Soft wadding

Needles for fine sewing

Sewing machine with zipper foot

Rectangular embroidery frame

Staples or drawing pins to apply the fabric to the frame (if a conventional frame is not available)

LEFT: *A sculptural surface has been created by means of felt tubes. The direction, length, width and colour of the three-dimensional lines developed from the gestural marks within the original painted study.*

BELOW: *Painting of Rhode Island chickens.*

Method

1 Make a tracing of the chosen animal or bird from a painting or photograph. Trace only the main divisions between one colour and the next.

2 Turn the tracing over and with a large needle poke holes on all the traced lines about 5mm (¼in) apart. In this way, the needle will enter the wrong side of the drawing which gives the right side of the tracing a rough texture not unlike a cheese grater (see page 40).

3 Lay this, with the rough texture of the tracing uppermost, on the right side of the piece of fabric.

4 Holding the tracing paper down firmly with one hand, take a small pad of felt in the other hand. Dab the felt into the French chalk and rub it gently and systematically through the holes, using a gentle circular movement.

5 Carefully remove the tracing paper. Rows of powder dots should now be visible.

6 Join these by using a fine paint brush and a water-based white paint. You will need to make many tiny strokes as the brush inevitably collects powder.

7 Mount this prepared fabric onto a frame. Attach a strong lining fabric to the frame to provide additional strength (see pages 172–3).

8 Now make a selection of piped felt tubes by cutting the felt into 3.5cm (1½in) strips to fit the number 3 cord, and 3cm (1¼in) strips to fit the number 2 cord.

9 Place the cord in the fold of the felt and using the zipper foot and shortest stitch length machine as close to the cord as possible in matching cotton.

10 Trim away the excess felt from the tube, close to the machine stitching. (In other projects the trim could be left on to provide a different effect.)

11 Take the cords out of the tubes and save them for making subsequent lengths. If a crisper, harder effect is required then leave the cord inside the tubes but the ends of the cord must be carefully trimmed back at the end of each tube.

12 Cut lengths of piped felt and shape their ends as required.

13 The finished chicken, as illustrated, was made by placing lengths of piped felt in groups of lines in the direction and to the same length as suggested by the gestural marks of the painting.

14 Sew the tubes to the ground fabric using a small stitch entering the cloth

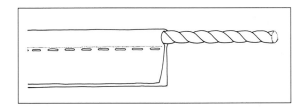

Step 9.

Step 1.

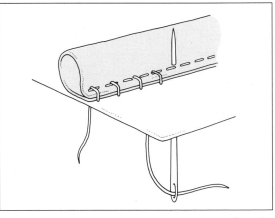

Step 14.

126

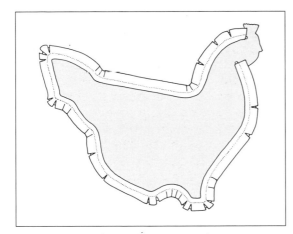

Decorated side facing (Steps 19–20).

from underneath (beside the fine line of machine stitching on the tube), passing through the underside of the tube just above the line of stitching on the tube and then re-entering the fabric. The distance between stitches depends on the scale of the work and the wear that it has to endure. For this small project the stitches were 5mm (¼in) apart.

15 It is important to overcast firmly the machine stitching at each end of a tube after it has been cut to length and shape. Notice that the ends of the tubes illustrated have been cut at different angles in order to conform to the confines of the area they are filling.

16 For the chicken's feet, cut 2 feet-shaped layers of felt for each foot. Using the zig-zag foot, zig-zag around the edge but leave the top of the leg open. Gently ease some wadding into the feet, using a knitting needle.

17 Remove the work from the frame and cut out the shape of the chicken according to the basic pattern; allow 1cm (½in) for turnings. A basic pattern may need scaling up or down to suit the particular requirement (see page 175).

18 Make a length of piping long enough to go all around the perimeter of the chicken, but do not trim; the excess will be required as a seam allowance.

19 Place this piped felt on the right side of the decorated section of the chicken with turnings facing the same direction.

20 Pin and tack. Snip any corners (as shown in the diagram). Stitch using the zipper foot.

21 Now turn the whole edge inwards and catch stitch; the piping will now form the actual edge.

22 Lay the legs in the appropriate position on the front body, with the top unsewn edge level with the turned edge. Secure with a few stitches.

23 Cut a piece of felt to match the shape of the decorated front (plus turnings).

24 Place the backing felt on the chicken. Carefully turn the seam allowance to the inside and closely slip stitch to the front. Leave a small gap at a point on the edge.

25 Fill with wadding.

26 Sew up the gap using small slip stitches.

Wrong side facing (Steps 21–2).

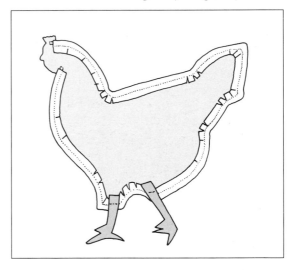

CREATING SURFACES

There is often a natural tendency to always draw and paint familiar subjects, such as landscapes and plants. However, unusual subjects can help one to break away, to look and think afresh and then to consider what could develop as a direct result of these drawings.

Here, bits of old engine parts formed the unlikely starting point. Preliminary sketching eventually led to images of selected aspects of the components, i.e. leaves of metal gave rise to drawings of a particular character.

Next emerged interpretations in fabrics: a series of samples showing ribbed, pleated, folded, linear and layered treatments. They are simple both in materials and techniques used – two fabrics plus the use of the twin needle on the sewing machine.

Any other medium could have been selected: clay, paper, wood, etc. But it is the simplicity of experimenting with limited methods and materials that yields success; without these limitations the results are rarely innovative and usually chaotic.

From these surface treatments a selection can be made and considered in the design of a finished article. The product could be a piece of clothing, an interior design or maybe a soft toy. In this case, a doll was the end result because it provided a complete, small-scale example of all the possibilities that could be integral to the decoration of a full-size garment.

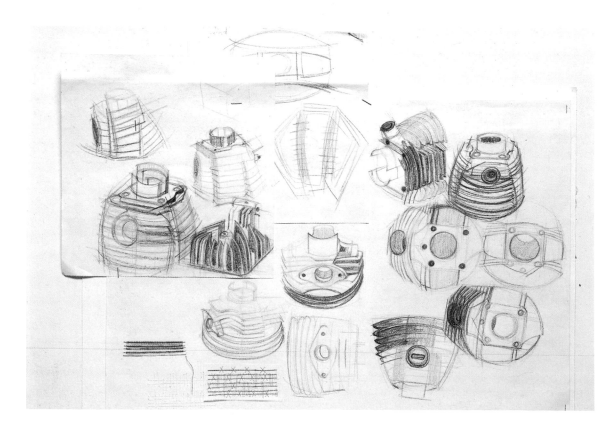

LEFT: *Simple sketches of engine parts were transposed to sketches in cloth.*

ABOVE: *The more the experiments in decorative effects, the greater will be the creative end result.*

DOLL

Materials
For the drawing:
A suitable subject
Pencils, chalks, crayons – almost anything
Drawing paper

For the cloth samples:
Sewing machine with a ¹⁄₁₂in twin needle (to be used with a 7-groove twin-needle foot)
A length of ordinary nylon net
A length of a thin, knitted, stretchy, non-frayable synthetic fabric. (A different result is achieved when working both across and with the grain.)
Any sewing or machine embroidery cotton (when comparing small reels remember that there is about five times the length on machine embroidery cotton). In these samples a contrast of colour has been used: DMC number 50 machine embroidery cotton; yellow 726, orange 740 and pink 776. One 500m reel of each
Scissors

For the doll:
Pattern for the doll. In this model the head was designed from the Kenyan heads shown on page 35. The pattern is included (see page 132).
    The body is like a small rectangular cushion 30.5 × 12.5cm (12 × 5in); the legs are 40.5cm (16in) long, 10cm (4in) round; the arms are 28cm (11in) long, 9cm (3½in) round
Fabric. A cotton curtain lining was used here. Make sure it is pre-shrunk
Matching sewing cotton
Sewing needles, plus a curved needle for attaching hair and eyes
Wadding (soft and fine)

LEFT: *Finished doll. Making small-scale clothes for dolls is a good starting point before progressing to more ambitious full-scale dressmaking. This decorative treatment of fabrics can also be applied to interior design for cushions, panels, hangings, etc.*

Lengths of decorated fabric selected from the most appropriate samples made here
Buttons or beads for the eyes. This doll has an old-fashioned flat, linen button on which a small embroidered one has been sewn
No pattern was used for the clothes as they were built up around the doll
Knitting needle

Method
To make some of the samples:
Prepare the machine for use with the twin needle by following instructions in machine handbook or by using this general guide.
1 Fill a spool and place it in position.
2 Take two reels of cotton, place one on each spindle. The two cottons should pass either side of the tension disc.
3 If the two reels are of different colours, it is much easier to make sure that the cottons are now threaded into the corresponding left and right needles.
4 The stitch length should be selected according to the effect desired.
5 The stitch width is normally straight, but on the net samples a very small swing has been set in order to slightly widen the line and make it a little more prominent. Do not use too wide a zig-zag or the needles might break.

For the net samples and particularly for the effect gained for the hair:
1 Sew nine rows of twin-needle stitching, with one groove between each row. Trim the net next to the outside row of stitching on each side.
2 Cut this length into 15cm (6in) pieces and fold in a zig-zag. Secure with a few hand stitches. You will need lots of these little units to make up the hair.
3 Continue to experiment until you have several samples.

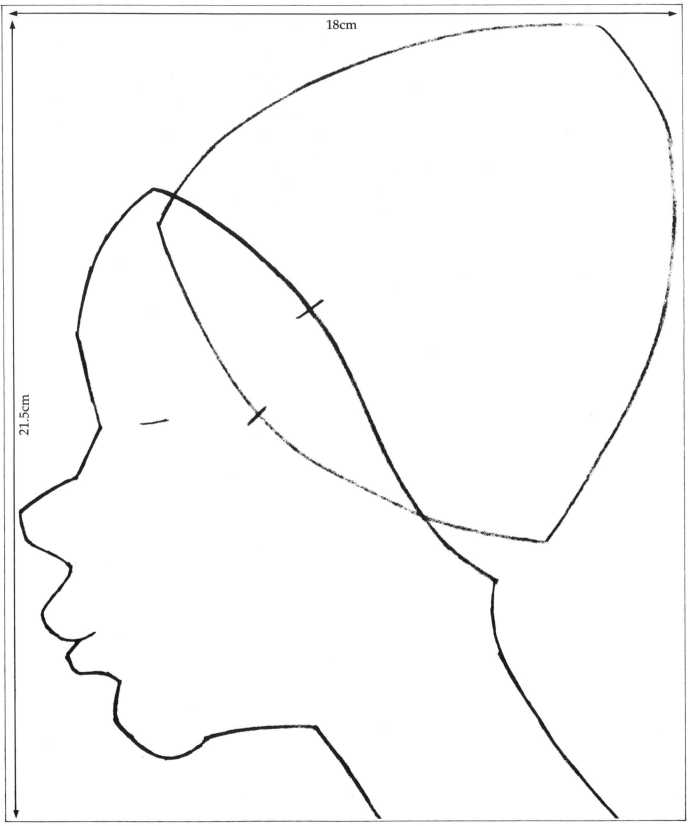

18cm

21.5cm

Pattern pieces for dolls head.

To make the (orange) knitted fabric samples:

1 Build up a combination of groove widths and colour changes in the cotton until you have a rich variety of samples.

2 The fabric can be further sculptured by using carefully placed gathering lines.

3 The wiggly braid effects can be achieved by making narrow strips of twin-needle sewing (four or five rows only). When these are trimmed close to the stitching on either side they will automatically curl and twist. They can be knotted or gathered as required. The same can be done with the net.

4 Experiment with different sizes of twin needle. A 5-groove foot is required for a $\frac{1}{8}$in needle and a 3-groove foot is required for a $\frac{1}{16}$in needle. Each produces a different scale of work and needs to be tried out in relation to the available fabric.

To make the doll:

1 Scale up the pattern to the required size (see page 175). Allow at least 5mm ($\frac{1}{4}$in) for turnings.

2 Cut out in fabric, reverse the pattern to cut the two pieces for the other sides.

3 Join one face portion to head section, matching notches. When both sides are ready, place them together, right sides facing.

4 Stitch all round but leave the base of the neck open for wadding. Using a knitting needle, ensure that the wadding reaches into all the tiny areas like the nose and the mouth. Fill the rest of the head and body.

5 Join all parts of the body together as if they were a set of linked, multi-shaped cushions.

6 Decorate the doll with a rich head of hair using the net samples. Make some wonderful clothes from fabric samples. Add plenty of necklaces and bangles from other pieces.

PART 2

APPLICATION

SECTION 7: LARGE SCALE WORKS FROM
PAINTINGS
SECTION 8: LARGE SCALE WORKS FROM
PHOTOGRAPHS

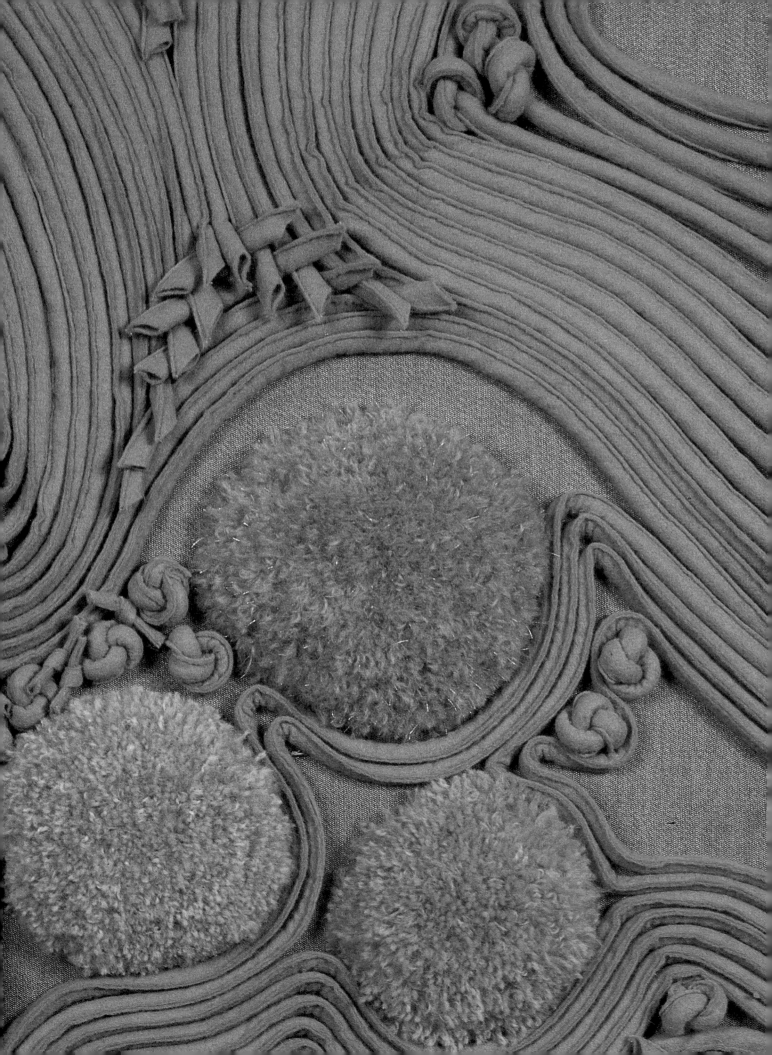

SECTION 7: LARGE SCALE WORKS FROM PAINTINGS

This section considers in greater depth how painting can be used to record and assimilate more complicated material as well as to assess the most appropriate technique for transposition of the image into fabric and thread. It shows how the techniques learnt in Part 1 can be applied to larger and more complex articles.

Despite their large scale, these three major projects are no more difficult to work than those already described. They are different in that they underline more critically the benefit and importance of sustained and organized preliminary art work. Continued discipline and systematic planning are fundamental to the success of a large-scale project.

PATCHWORK BEDSPREAD

This large patchwork in Viyella was sewn by hand because of the irregular nature of the shapes which are based on poinsettias.

The technique is exactly that used for both the waistcoat and the sweater (see pages 110–119). The only differences are the introduction of a representational image and the scale of the work.

The method still begins with a small painting, this one was 38 × 28cm (15 × 11in), which was then enlarged (see page 175) to 2.38 × 2.08m (94 × 82in).

Viyella of varying colours was used as the fabric. Using one type of material throughout helps to keep the work even when working over a large area. For a bedspread you need to choose a fabric that is firm yet soft and lightweight so that it can easily be washed or dry-cleaned. It is also wise to check that all materials are pre-shrunk.

The method of patchwork used (see page 112) when all turnings are attached to the interlining, helps to keep the article in good shape, even when heavily used.

This bedspread has been made up as for a wall hanging (see pages 178) and includes twenty hanging sleeves at the top end so that it can be hung.

Bedspread: traditional English patchwork.

Line and wash painting of poinsettias.

Tracing and preparation for enlargement of the poinsettias.

A large walk-through appliqué hanging answers a specific design problem – it provides a division between two rooms where a conventional door could not be built. Decoration of doorways can be found in many countries, particularly in India where there are many fine examples of embroidered torans.

MACHINE APPLIQUÉ CURTAIN

The curtain is 3.36m (11ft) high and is made up of furnishing fabrics of many kinds: velvets, Dupions and corduroys, which have then been applied to a heavy wool ground.

The work started with a series of paintings in the same way as the appliqué picture on page 27. The subject here was a group of apple trees in full fruit. The more complex the subject, the more experimental paintings will be required.

BELOW AND FOLLOWING TWO PAGES: *A series of paintings of apple trees: the starting point for the curtain.*

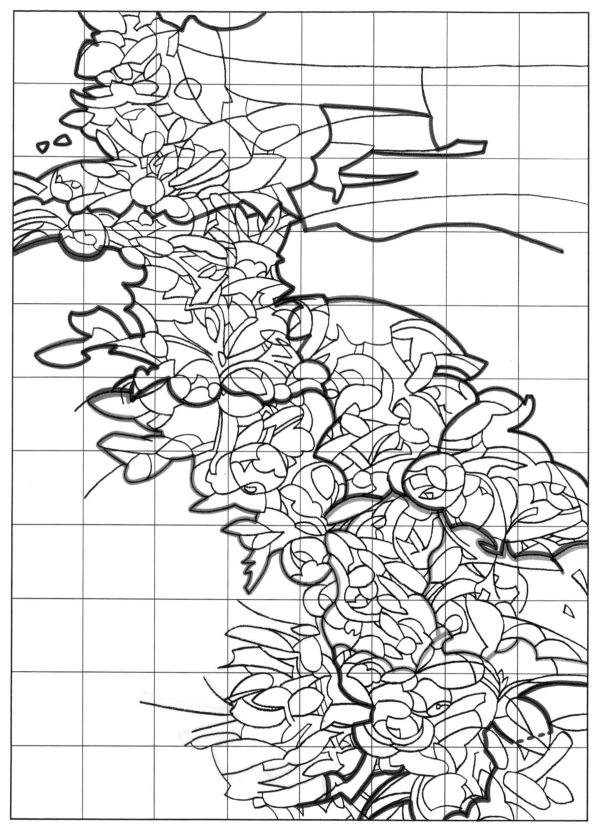

Tracing of apple trees. It has been divided into seven manageable areas, marked in different coloured felt-tipped pens, and squared up for enlargement.

144

After careful consideration, select the aspect you wish to develop and then make a careful tracing. Because of the scale of the work, the tracing will have to be further divided into manageable areas. (These areas can be marked in different coloured felt-tipped pens.)

After the tracing has been enlarged these areas relate to a patch of appliqué of a size that can comfortably be handled in one piece on the sewing machine.

The method of making up is as described on pages 26–7, but here a series of autonomous appliqué sections were made which eventually interlock to complete the image.

When all the sections are made place them in position on the ground area and secure by hand stitching around the entire edge of each silhouette. Some further holding stitches will also be necessary across the middle of the large sections of appliqué.

The central split of this curtain was cut after the appliqué was complete; the raw edges were then bound with a strip of bias in a matching fabric to the ground cloth.

The hanging was interlined with the heaviest Vilene (sometimes known as pelmet Vilene) and finally lined with curtain lining (see page 178).

The bottom edge of this work was shaped to fit over three brick steps at the base of the door arch (see page 140).

Twenty-one hanging sleeves set close together across the 2.44m (8ft) width have proved sufficient to carry the full weight of the curtain.

Detail of appliqué.

KNEELERS AND ALTAR CUSHIONS

The most important factor in this church project was that the chosen design should relate to its environment which was historic and timeless. The kneelers had to blend and belong and yet become the jewels in an already ornate setting.

The paintings were made after first studying the pattern already existing in the thirteenth century stonework within St Anne's Chapel. They were also strongly influenced by the dominant feature of the chapel: the stained glass roundels within the slender fenestration. Finding the patterns and choosing the colours was fairly easy and reflected what was already present. The final design solution took shape by reiterating the dominance of the circular window motifs together with their existing scarlet and blue.

The decision then was how the embroidery should be carried out. It had to be hard wearing and technically simple enough for a group to embroider from the simple paintings, samples and basic instructions provided. Durable but fine Wilton carpet thrums were worked on a twelve hole to the inch canvas (2.5cm). The main body of the hassock was made in cowhide to limit the amount of fine work. It was also the practical solution to the problem of everyday wear and tear. Scarlet cowhide was used with blues, fawns and buffs for the embroidery, thereby repeating the visual sensation initially created by the windows.

 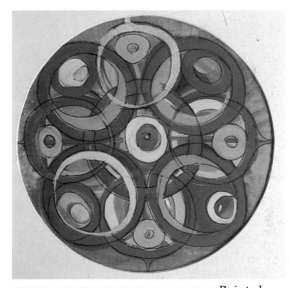

LEFT: *Kneelers and altar cushions designed for St Anne's Chapel, Lincoln Cathedral. They were designed to complement both the existing colours in the cathedral and the architectural details.*

ABOVE AND FOLLOWING TWO PAGES: *Painted designs based on architectural details within St Anne's Chapel. Note the great diversity of shapes expressed within the same theme.*

Originally there were twelve designs but one was lost. The designs had to be repeated twice: for a second set of kneelers and for the circular embroideries to be incorporated along the altar rail cushion.

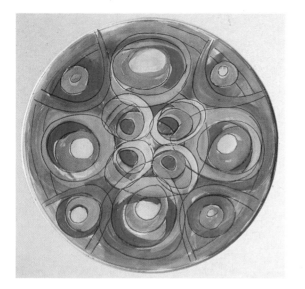

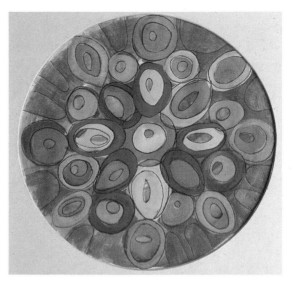

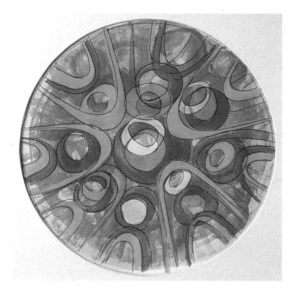

RIGHT: *Window in St Anne's Chapel; the inspiration for the shape and colours of the kneelers.*

*Tent, knotted and velvet stitches were chosen for
the embroidery because they are hardwearing.
They also achieve a low-relief effect.*

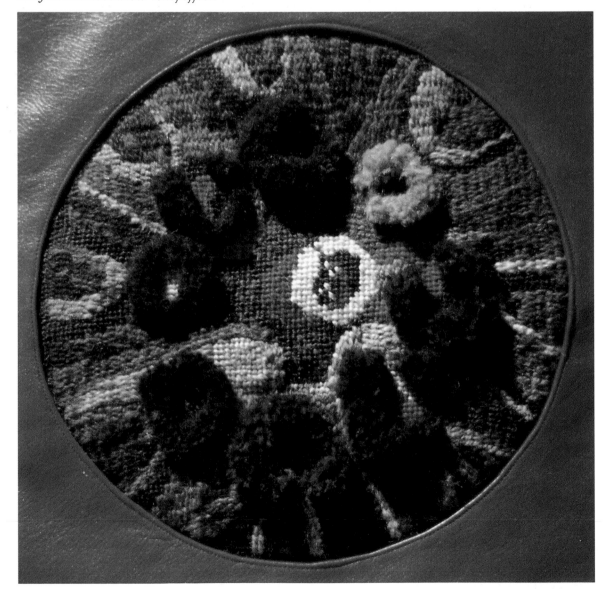

*Finished hassock: 40.5cm (16in) wide, 25.5cm
(10in) across, 9cm (3½in) deep. Once the
embroidery was complete and stretched, the
hassocks were made up by a professional
upholsterer.*

SECTION 8: LARGE SCALE WORKS FROM PHOTOGRAPHS

Stimulus and inspiration for the designs in this section come mainly from photographs either taken by the designer or, in the case of some commissioned work, supplied by the client.

Photography is a more immediate method of recording visual material than painting but one that can lack the flexibility of the critical human eye in selecting, rejecting or highlighting certain concepts or details.

All the techniques have been introduced elsewhere in the book – appliqué, felt relief and loop pile – but here they are used on a grander scale and require a much more systematic approach.

DECORATIVE PANEL

Detail of decorative panel.

Strict adherence to the geological colours was an essential part of the design brief and provided the linear structure of the embroidery.

The techniques used were those described on pages 126–7.

The felt piping has been reproduced as for the soft toy (see also pages 126–7). The differences here are that several sizes of piping cord have been combined; the trim has been left on; the cord has sometimes been used as a gathering string and the trimmed piped felt has often been applied with the stitched, trimmed edge uppermost.

The tufted 'oil seam' has been made by using a rich colour mixture of stranded cottons in combination with a loop pile tool (see page 86).

Also included amongst the 120 DMC skeins of cotton is some machine embroidery thread with a metallic and lustrous finish (see page 182).

RIGHT: *A low-relief panel in felt and loop pile: the lines and colours developed from rock samples and sonor drawings of the east–west section through Beryl A oil field.*

PAIR OF DECORATIVE PANELS

The same techniques were applied in constructing this pair of panels.

They developed from a series of photographs of Japanese gardens.

Pair of low-relief panels: 91cm (36in) high, 56cm (22in) wide.

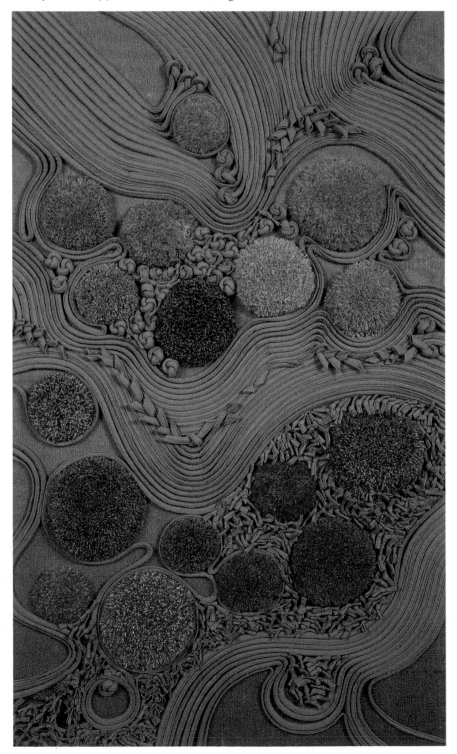

The camera images have not been slavishly copied but instead the bare essence has been extracted. The work reveals only sensations of gentle colour, raked gravel, combed moss and meticulously clipped Sharenbai bushes.

FOLDING SCREENS

The two folding screens have also been inspired by photographs; the first by photos of koi carp (the shapes they create in movement, their variety of colour and their individuality of form), and the second by photos of seagulls at feeding time.

These folding screens were produced to show representational subjects in the simplest technique of all – appliqué. The style of work was chosen to demonstrate its suitability to interior decoration, particularly where a wall panel is not appropriate.

Various images were traced from different photographs and moved about on a plain white sheet of paper to achieve a new composition. They were selected, rejected, positioned and re-positioned to achieve an overall balance.

When the group of tracings were placed satisfactorily, one single tracing was made. This established the basis of the design and yet still allowed any number of changes to be made by re-tracing the last of the overlay drawings. The embroidery technique used was exactly as described on pages 26–7.

These final tracings for the fish and bird screens
show the incorporation of related side panels.
The images from the centre flow out laterally but
still make a complete area within any one frame.

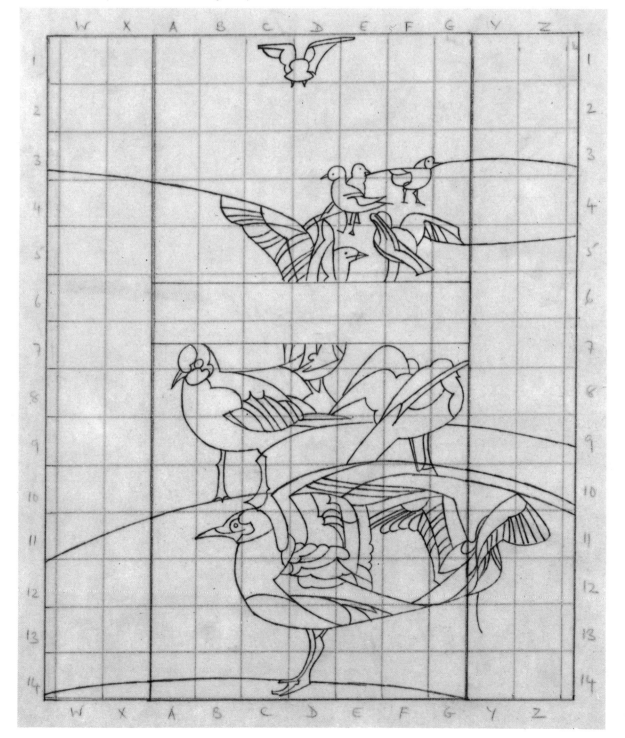

Both works depend on very few fabrics: the variety of surface is mainly achieved by the subtle changes of colour afforded by the grain of Dupions, velvets and moirés.

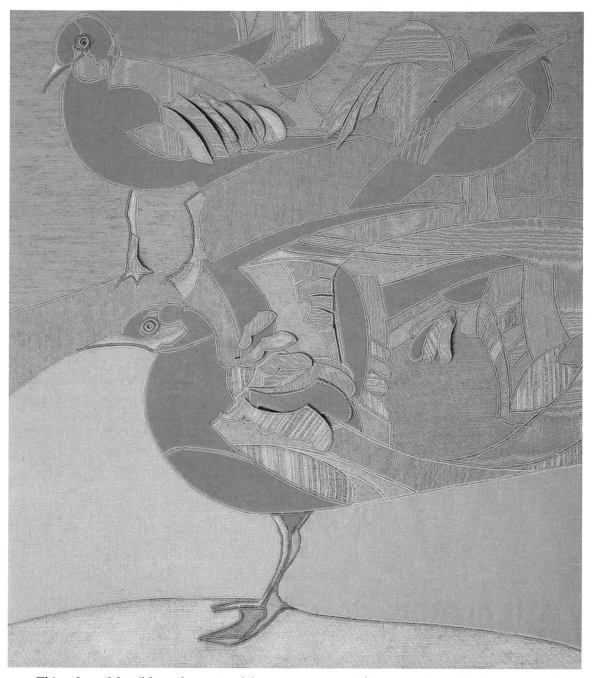

LEFT: *This enlarged detail from the centre of the screen shows the simple appliqué technique which in some parts forms additional sections raised from the surface in low relief.*

ABOVE: *This screen shows the same approach as for the fish screen but is different in terms of colour and in the basic division of area. For example, this detail shows much smaller raised sections. The overall size of both screens is the same, 1.52m (60in) high.*

CHASUBLE, STOLE, BURSE AND VEIL

The matching chasuble, stole, burse and veil are straightforward and simple – one colour, one kind of fabric and one technique.

LEFT: *Simplicity was the aim of this project. The minimal statement is the result of using no elaborate materials or traditional techniques.*

ABOVE: *Detail of chasuble.*

The client's specification demanded simply that the 'decoration' should be reminiscent of earth, air, fire and water. The design is therefore a simple statement in low relief line (using the techniques described on pages 126–7) based on a detail abstracted from a collection of photographs of different wood grains.

Different wood grains provided the basis for the design of the chasuble, stole, burse and veil.

One other design constraint was that the motif had to be suitable for extension and variation to make three further sets in the other liturgical colours of gold, green and purple.

If you are attempting church embroidery for the first time you should consult a good basic book such as Beryl Dean's *Embroidery in Religion and Ceremonial* (see Further Reading, page 182).

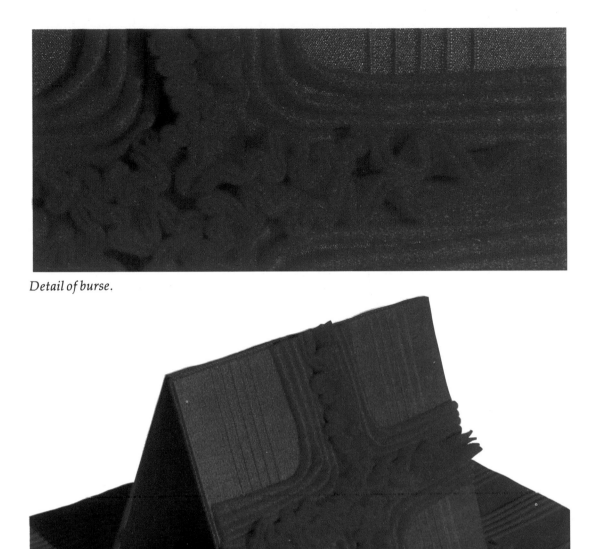

Detail of burse.

Burse and veil.

PART 3
THREADS, EQUIPMENT AND TECHNIQUES

SECTION 9: THREADS

There are so many kinds of thread that it would be almost impossible to provide a comprehensive list.

It is always best to design around what is readily and easily available, leaving the acquisition of the unusual to particular opportunities when they arise.

Threads can be divided into two distinct groups: those that are made especially for embroidery and those that are really designed for weaving, knitting, lace making, carpet manufacture, dressmaking, and soft furnishing – the gimps, bouclés, braids, thrums, etc. The vast range of yarns available is interchangeable between the crafts. In addition to the specifically designed yarns there are special materials like raffia, ribbon and chenille which cross many disciplines.

Basic embroidery thread, which should be available in most craft shops, is of several types.

1 Stranded cotton. This is made up of six fine, lustrous, soft threads which can be easily separated and used singly or in any combination. Over 300 colours are available.

2 Perlé. Also cotton and shiny, but non-stranded. Comes in three weights 8 (fine), 5 (medium) and 3 (thick). Available in about 400 colours, including rainbow mixtures.

3 Laine tapisserie or tapestry wool. A soft, 4 ply with many uses. Nearly 500 colours are available.

4 Retors à broder (now Retors mat). A non-stranded, matt, fairly thick cotton supplied in over 200 beautiful colours.

5 Coton à broder. A matt cotton but with some lustre, much finer than retors à broder and also non-stranded.

These five threads are all made by DMC, but most have very fine British and German equivalents made by Coats and Madeira.

6 Broder Medicis. This is a beautiful range of fine wool made by DMC. Comes in a range of over 100 very subtle shades. The nearest British equivalent is the superb and well-known Appleton crewel wool.

7 Machine embroidery cotton. DMC produce a series of embroidery cottons on large and small reels in weights of 30 and 50 in a good range of over 200 colours. They also produce about 30 colours in rainbow shades.

There are lots of other embroidery threads such as gold, silver and metals which give an enormous choice when specific techniques and results are required.

PRECEDING PAGES: *A small selection from the enormous range of DMC threads.*

170

SECTION 10: EQUIPMENT

NEEDLES

Of the many kinds of sewing needles available, each is suited to a particular aspect of any work that may be undertaken. The most usual and useful needles are listed here.

1 Sharps. These are essential for all fine sewing. They are small eyed and sharp pointed.

2 Crewel. The most versatile and the most commonly used embroidery needle. Comes in many sizes but its great advantage is the long-shaped eye which can carry varying amounts and thicknesses of thread.

3 Chenille. These have a long, large eye and a sharp point. They can carry thick threads without damaging the fabric and should be used when a crewel needle is too small.

4 Tapestry. These look like a chenille needle but have a blunt point. They are useful for fabrics like canvas where it is important not to catch the threads of the ground fabric with a sharp point.

5 Beading. These are longer and much finer than the average needle. The finest is hard to distinguish from a hair. They are essential if small beads are to be applied to the work.

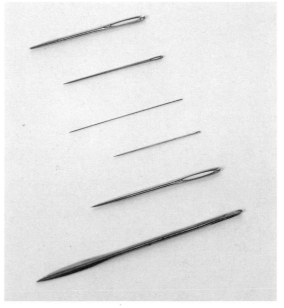

Needles (from top to bottom): tapestry, crewel, beading, sharp, chenille, packing.

6 Packing. These have a spear-shaped point which enables them to carry string or other substantial thread through a fabric without tearing it.

SCISSORS

Three kinds are usually essential for embroidery.

1 Embroidery scissors. These are small, pointed and very sharp. They are essential for cutting tiny shapes in fabric and for all small-scale trimming of threads.

2 Cutting-out scissors or shears. It would be impossible to manage without these when cutting out fabric of any size.

3 Paper scissors. It is important to set aside a pair of scissors for paper cutting. Paper definitely blunts most good-quality scissors. However, the designers of the true Finnish Fiskars made by Wilkinson, boast that their scissors can be used for paper and that they never become blunt.

FRAMES

Many people prefer to work without a frame of any kind. Sometimes this is because the opportunity to use one has never arisen and sometimes because the advantages of using frames have never been explained.

Many kinds of embroidery are, with practice, easier to do on a frame, particularly most types of surface stitchery and all canvas work embroidery. The big advantage of using a frame is that the work remains unpuckered and the ground fabric does not become distorted. This greatly reduces the task of stretching the work when it is finished. Another advantage is that it is much quicker to sew on a ground fabric that is taut and always in place rather than on one which has to be continually adjusted and re-positioned. Also, both hands are free to embroider, one above and one below the work.

There are two kinds of frame, circular and rectangular. The circular, hoop or tambour frame is the most commonly used. They used to be made only of wood but are now available in a metal which looks like the material of Aero knitting needles. Round frames are essential for many kinds of free machine embroidery and are also useful for certain surface stitchery techniques.

Many people consider the metal frame better than the wooden variety for machine embroidery. This is because, when stretching the fabric across the frame, it can be held much more tightly than in a wooden frame. This absolute tautness of the cloth preparatory to machine embroidery is important, otherwise the cotton will continually break. However, one advantage of the wooden frame is that with difficult or delicate fabrics, tissue paper, tape or gauze can be used to wrap the inner frame, thereby softening it against the fabric. This fine adjustment would not be possible with the metal hoop because it is manufactured with a concave groove in the inner ring in which the outer ring must sit.

When preparing a wooden frame for machine embroidery it is important to make absolutely sure that the fabric is resting on the machine bed and not suspended, however slightly, just above. Check that the *inner* hoop is actually a fraction lower than the outer one. If the outer hoop is touching the machine bed then almost certainly the fabric, which is stretched over the inner hoop, will not be resting flat on the work surface. The fabric must be as taut as a drum and must not be bouncing between the hoop and the machine bed, otherwise the thread will break with monotonous regularity.

A simple rectangular frame can easily be made from four pieces of wood joined together with screw-on, flat, metal angle brackets. An old picture frame can also be used.

However, if something a little more refined is wanted there are numerous types of professional slate frame available. These have the great advantages of

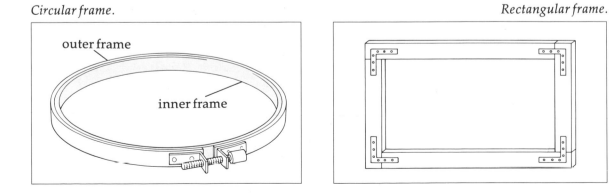

Circular frame.

outer frame

inner frame

Rectangular frame.

allowing adjustments to the tautness of the work to be made and of storing all the parts of the piece that are not actually being worked on the two roller sides.

Fabrics that are expensive and/or delicate and too small to fit across the frame should be attached with large holding stitches to a support fabric backing *after* the backing has been stretched onto the frame.

To attach the actual fabric to be worked or the backing fabric to a simple, home-made frame, first stretch and attach one edge of the fabric along one side of the frame using staples or drawing pins. Do the same on the opposite side pulling the cloth tight and even. Attach the other two sides making sure that the surface is taut and uniform.

If the fabric is likely to fray then make sure that the edges are turned or overcast with machine stitching. In the case of canvas it is essential to wrap each raw edge with either masking tape or a strip of fabric. If using fabric then it must be stitched.

To attach the backing fabric or canvas to a slate frame follow these steps:

1 Bind or secure the edges of all fabrics. This prevents fraying and lends added strength to the edges for the later process of lacing.

2 Plan the project so that the two opposite sides of the fabric do not exceed the length of the strips of the webbing on the rollers.

3 Taking each roller in turn (webbing attached) mark the centre of each piece of webbing.

4 Mark the centre of each of the two edges of fabric to be attached to the webbing.

5 Place the upper sides of the webbing and the right sides of the fabric together, matching the two sets of centre marks, and pin.

6 Working from the centre points outwards, sew the fabric to the webbing with small overcasting stitches using strong sewing cotton.

7 When both rollers are attached to opposite sides of the ground cloth, roll each inwards until all the excess fabric has been absorbed.

8 Place slats through the slots of the rollers and push apart as tightly as possible.

9 Drop in the pegs.

10 Using a packing needle and fine string, lace the remaining two free edges to the slats. Secure the string.

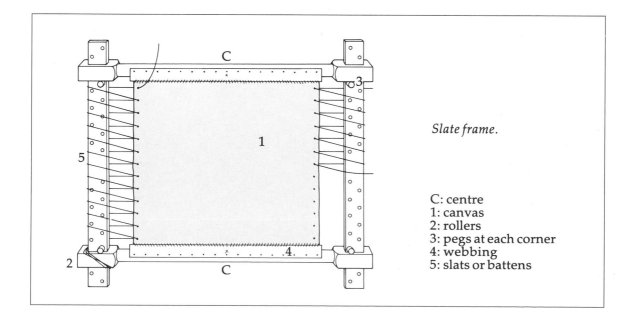

Slate frame.

C: centre
1: canvas
2: rollers
3: pegs at each corner
4: webbing
5: slats or battens

SEWING MACHINES

There are many sewing machine manufacturers producing models that vary considerably in quality and price. The most important consideration when choosing a machine is that it has versatility, so it should be electric and have a swing needle in addition to normal straight stitching.

Most embroiderers do not like or need elaborate machines with built-in computers which can produce complex patterns – a quality, reliable machine is what is required and the manufacturers Bernina, Pfaff and Elna have good reputations.

A sewing machine should not be bought in a hurry. It is important to actually try sewing with the particular machine under consideration. If necessary, take some of your own fabric into the shop and try it on the machines or, if possible, borrow one or two models for a short period so you can try them at home in a realistic and calm environment.

OTHER USEFUL ITEMS

STAPLER OR STAPLE GUN
An office stapler that opens out is very useful for attaching fabric to frames. It is not as robust as a staple gun but it has the advantage of being a great deal cheaper.

STANLEY KNIFE
Essential for cutting card or preparing mounts.

STEEL RULER or STEEL-EDGED WOODEN RULER
Necessary for use with a very sharp cutting knife.

HAMMER and PLIERS

SECTION 11: HOW TO ENLARGE A DESIGN

1 Draw a rectangle around the design to determine the actual dimensions.
2 Divide the design into squares and label with letters on one edge and numbers on another.
3 If you do not want to draw squares on the actual design, first make a tracing and then divide this into squares.
4 If the design is intricate it will require small squares of about 2.5cm (1in).
5 Decide how much larger the work has to be; at least on one of the dimensions.
6 Find or tape together a piece of paper big enough to carry the enlarged design.
7 Lay the small drawing on the larger sheet of paper so that one of its corners corresponds to the same corner on the enlargement.

8 Draw a diagonal line (AB) through the design.
9 Decide on the eventual width of the enlargement and extend AC to D.
10 Extend the diagonal AB until it meets the perpendicular from D, at point E. Thus DE is the new height.
11 Complete the rest of the rectangle in similar fashion.
12 Remove the design in order to divide this new rectangle ADEF into squares. The number of squares must be the same as in the small rectangle ACBG. Numbering and lettering should also correspond.
13 Now, square by square, the lines of the small design have to be transposed to the larger squares.

The same process can be applied for reducing a design.

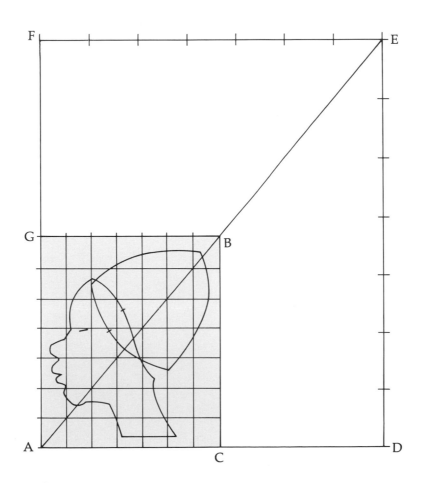

SECTION 12: FINISHING

STRETCHING

Stretching an embroidery is an essential stage if you want to achieve a perfect finish. Pressing with an iron is acceptable and appropriate in certain circumstances but the following method achieves re-shaping where necessary, removes all crinkles from the embroidered surface and allows even the tightest, most dense work to remain raised and crisp.

1 Lay several layers of blotting paper on a drawing board or an old wooden surface.
2 Thoroughly wet the blotting paper with water.
3 Lay the work on it, face upwards.

4 Starting at the centre of one edge, gently but firmly press in drawing pins at about 2.5cm (1in) intervals; the pins must be secure but do not be tempted to hit them with a hammer because the spike will simply part company from the head.
5 Pull the opposite side of the work, making sure the fabric grain is straight, and insert a further row of drawing pins.
6 Treat the other edges in the same way, continuing to add pins until there are no wrinkles left.
7 Allow to dry overnight in a warm place before removing the pins.

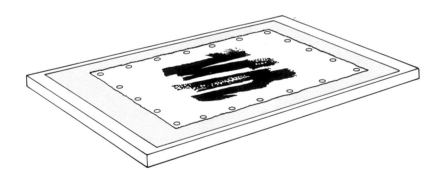

HOW TO PREPARE WORK FOR A WALL PANEL

There are two methods, but in both cases the work should be stretched as on the facing page.

1 Small pieces of work can be laced with fine string over cardboard or mounting board using a packing needle. The fabric turnings should not be too small. However, if the edge to be turned is narrow or fragile then it should first be strengthened by the addition of a binding or stitching (or both).

2 The second method is suitable for any size work. The work should be stretched over a wooden frame and stapled on the back edge. The frame for larger work will need the addition of one or more central bearers. For any size of wooden stretcher frame it is a great advantage to have extra wooden wedges in the corners. (Wedges should be inserted after the work has been stretched.) The 90° corner does *not* go against the frame. If it does, the wedges will continually drop out. One or two firm taps with the hammer are usually enough to secure the wedges.

This method of supporting the work is the most perfect and accurate if the work is to go to a professional picture framer.

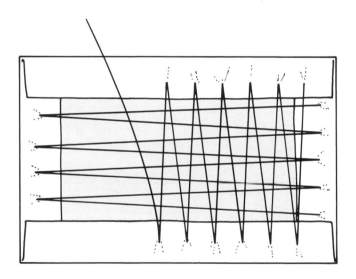

Lacing a small piece of work.

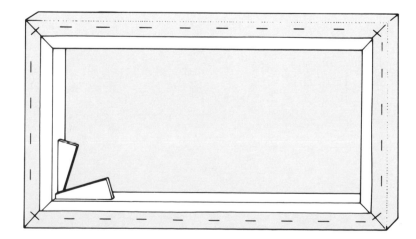

Stretching over a wooden frame.

HOW TO PREPARE WORK FOR A CURTAIN OR HANGING

This method is ideal for making up embroideries which need to drape softly to show off their full effect.

1 Stretch or press the embroidery.

2 Cut an interlining to the size required for the finished work. A non-woven fabric like Vilene is usually best.

3 Lay this on the back of the work in the exact position of the finished shape required.

4 Gently bring all the raw edges of the embroidery over the interlining, and pin. Snip the curved edges.

5 Carefully stitch all these turnings to the interlining using a herringbone stitch (see page 82). Be careful not to catch any of the front material.

6 Cut a lining the size of the finished article adding 1.5cm (⅝in) turnings all round.

7 Lay this on the back of the work. Turn in raw edges allowing just a little of the front fabric to show. Pin in place and slip stitch invisibly to the work.

If fabric loops or sleeves are needed for suspending the work, continue as follows:

8 Decide on the length, width and number of loops required.

9 Cut a length of matching fabric twice the required length (plus turnings) and the required width (plus turnings).

10 Cut a length of interlining the exact width of the loop but add 5cm (2in) to each end for securing to the inside of the work.

11 Turn the edges of the fabric over and line exactly as for the main work.

12 Fold the finished loop over and attach to the back of the work *before attaching the lining at the top.*

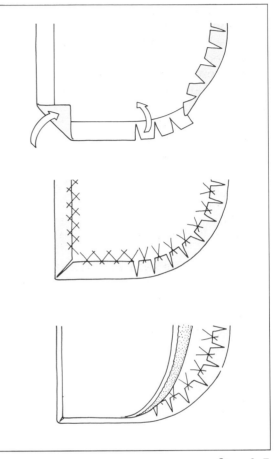

Steps 3–7.

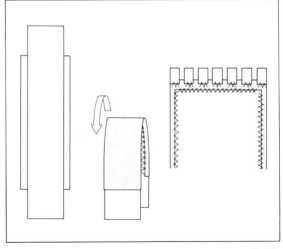

Steps 8–12.

HOW TO CUT A MOUNT

The smartest, simplest and quickest type of mount is the 'window' mount. These can be used to place one superb piece of finished work into a quick state of presentation, to gather together a group of sketches or samples or to make a greetings card.

A well-cut mount can also be used by the picture framer.

Materials

Card or mounting board; there are many weights, types and colours to choose from

Stanley knife or other craft knife

Steel ruler

Piece of waste card or a cutting mat on which to do the cutting (necessary to protect the table, the knife and the quality of the cut). Cutting mats are expensive but invaluable in the long term

HB pencil

Rubber (soft)

Pin

Sticky tape

Method

1 Trim the work to 1cm (½in) of the required finished shape.

2 Lay the work on the card or mounting board. Seek a suitable position for a single motif. It is often better to have a slightly smaller border of card at the top than at the bottom. Depending on the purpose of the mount the side borders can either be of an equal width or, as in the case of a greetings card, be of different sizes.

3 With a pin, gently make four holes in the work at the points where each corner of the window will be. These must be accurate. Move the work out of the way and join these pin holes with a pencil line to denote the cutting line. These lines should be light and their positions rechecked by measurement.

4 Alternatively, make pencil marks instead of pin holes. With a pencil and ruler

Simple window mounted embroideries make effective greetings cards.

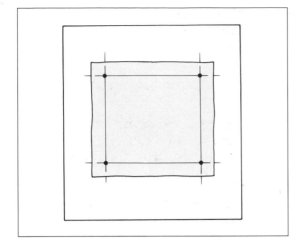

Steps 3–5.

make short light lines on the card which correspond to the continuation of the lines which indicate the eventual position of the window on the work.

5 Remove the work and join these lines. When the mount is cut these additional pencil lines can be carefully rubbed out.
6 Place the card over a suitably protected surface and using a steel rule cut along the marked lines.

It is a good idea not to attempt to cut all the way through the card in one movement but rather to make the first cut a positive groove into which subsequent greater pressure can be more accurately applied.

7 Take the work and place a little piece of sticky tape on the reverse of each side allowing about 1cm (½in) to protrude.
8 With the right side of the work facing, lower the mount in place and press firmly.
9 Turn the work over and tape all four edges properly.
10 Place a lining paper on the back, if required.

Any shape of mount can be cut, from simple squares and rectangles to intricate windows which follow the edges of more complicated work. Circles can be drawn and cut using a set of compasses specially designed to carry a knife. It is also worth considering the many different colours, types and weights of card.

Finally, when your standard of cutting is accurate and assured try using a knife blade designed to produce the deep bevelled (sloped) edges found in professionally cut mounts.

HOW TO MAKE A TWISTED CORD

Twisted cords can be a useful trim for an article where the colour and type of yarn would otherwise be very hard to match.
1 Decide on the final length of the cord required.
2 Take two pieces of thread three times this length.
3 Secure both ends together (one may well be a fold).
4 Hook one end around a door knob (or something similar) and stand at a distance holding the other end and keeping the cord taut.
5 Put a pencil between the two thicknesses of thread and rotate until the two are well twisted together.
6 Hold securely and fold half way along the twisted yarn.

7 Release the end on the door knob and place it firmly with the end still in the hand.
8 Allow the two to twirl together until they stop and a good cord is evident.
9 If the cord is very long, place a heavy object (like a large pair of scissors) on the centre fold at stage 6. Stand at the top of the stairs and allow the twizzle to complete itself. A second pair of hands would be even more helpful!

In the cord for the stool-top cushion (page 50) eight strands of Medici wool were used before folding, making a finished thickness of sixteen strands in all.

SUPPLIERS' LIST

DMC SUPPLIERS

FRANCE
Dollfus Mieg & Cie, 50 bd. de Sebastopol, 75139 Paris, Cedex 03.
AUSTRALIA
DMC Needlecraft Pty Ltd, 99–101 Lakemba Street, Belmore, NSW 2192.
AUSTRIA
Donaulandische Garngesellschaft Mbh, Tiefer Graben 23, 1013 Vienna.
BELGIUM
Dollfus Mieg & Cie SA, 13 rue de l'Intendant, 1210 Brussels.
COLOMBIA
Centraltex SA, Apartado Aereo 1498, Medellin.
DENMARK
Dollfus Mieg & Cie AS, Dampfaergevej 8 Frihavnen, 2100 Copenhagen.
ITALY
Dollfus Mieg EC SA, Viale Italia 84, 20020 Lainate, Milan.
JAPAN
DMC KK, Akasaka, PO Box 47, DF Building 8-go 2, 2-Chome Minami Aoyama Minato-Ku, Tokyo 10.
PANAMA
Centraltex SA, Apartado 1100, Zona 3, Colon.
PORTUGAL
Sociedade Luso-Francesa de Linhas LDA, Travessa da Escola, Araujo 36 A, Lisbon.
SOUTH AFRICA
SATC, 56 Barrack Street, PO Box 3868, Cape Town 8000.
SPAIN
Distribuidora Hilaturas Francesas SA, Caspe 30, 08010 Barcelona.
SWITZERLAND
Dollfus Mieg & Co SA, Zweignierderdassung, 9242 Oberuzwil.
UNITED KINGDOM
Dunlicraft Ltd, Pullman Road, Leicester LE8 2DY.
USA
The DMC Corporation, 107 Trumbull Street, Elizabeth NJ 07206.

JOURNALS

A very comprehensive and up-to-date list of stockists of embroidery supplies is always displayed in the following journals:
AUSTRALIA
Craft Australia, 100 George Street, Sydney, Australia. (Quarterly journal of the Crafts Council of Australia.)
CANADA
Embroidery Canada, 13491–101A Avenue, Surrey, BC, Canada V3T 1M4. (Journal of Embroiderers' Association of Canada Inc.)
NETHERLANDS
Textiel, Laan van Meerdervoort 300a, 2563 AL 's-Gravenhage, Netherlands.
NEW ZEALAND
Threads, 171 The Ridgeway, Mornington, Wellington 2, New Zealand. (Six-monthly magazine of Association of New Zealand Embroiderers' Guilds Inc.)
UNITED KINGDOM
Crafts, 8 Waterloo Place, London SW1Y 4AT. (Bi-monthly journal of The Crafts Council.)
Embroidery, PO Box 42B, East Molesey, Surrey KT8 9BB. (Quarterly.)
USA
The Flying Needle, 109 Timberwood Drive, Mars, PA16046, USA. (Quarterly journal of National Standards Council of American Embroiderers.)
Needle Arts, PO Box 305, Ridgefield, CT06877, USA. (Quarterly journal Embroiderers' Guild of America.)

SPECIALIST SUPPLIERS

ALEXANDER DESIGNS, Oast Cottage, Park Lane, Kemsing, Sevenoaks, Kent TN15 6NU. Loop pile tufting needle.
BOROVICK FABRICS LIMITED, 16 Berwick Street, London W1V 4HP. Unusual theatrical fabrics.
ELLS AND FARRIER, 20 Princes Street, London W1R 8PH. Beads and sequins.
MacCULLOCH AND WALLIS, 25/26 Dering Street, London W1R 0BH. Every kind of lining, interlining (including Dowlas), Bondaweb, piping cords, milliner's glue, etc.
RIBBON DESIGNS, 42 Lake View, Edgware, Middlesex HA8 7RU. Narrow ribbon (1.5mm) in over 60 colours.
SILKEN STRANDS, 33 Linksway, Gatley, Cheadle, Cheshire SK8 4LA. Shiny, silky, lurex and chenille threads.

SUPPLIERS IN USA

CERULEAN BLUE LIMITED, PO Box 21168 Seattle, WA 98111–3168. A complete international resource for textile art supplies.

FURTHER READING

Butler, Anne *The Batsford Encyclopaedia of Embroidery Stitches*, Batsford, 1979.
Clabburn, Pamela *The Needleworker's Dictionary*, Macmillan, 1976.
Colby, Avril *Patchwork*, Batsford, 1958.
Dean, Beryl *Embroidery in Religion and Ceremonial*, Batsford, 1981.
Itten, Johannes *The Art of Colour*, Van Nostrand Reinhold, 1961.
Itten, Johannes *Design and Form: the Basic Course at the Bauhaus*, Thames and Hudson, 1964.
Klein, Bernat *Design Matters*, Secker and Warburg, 1976.
Pye, David *The Nature and Art of Workmanship*, Cambridge University Press, 1968.

Risley, Christine *Machine Embroidery: a Complete Guide*, Studio Vista, 1973, paperback 1979.
Springall, Diana *Canvas Embroidery*, Batsford, 1969.
Thomas, Mary *Mary Thomas's Dictionary of Embroidery Stitches*, Hodder and Stoughton, 1934.
Thomas, Mary *Mary Thomas's Embroidery Book*, Hodder and Stoughton, 1936.
Whyte, Kathleen *Design in Embroidery*, Batsford, 1969.